HAUNTEI
IN EN(

BY

ELLIOT O'DONNELL

AUTHOR OF

"SOME HAUNTED HOUSES OF ENGLAND AND WALES"
"TWENTY YEARS' EXPERIENCE AS A GHOST HUNTER"
ETC. ETC.

PREFACE

IN presenting this volume to the Public, I wish to emphasise the fact that all the names of people and houses mentioned in it (saving in Chapter X.), in connection with the hauntings, are fictitious.

ELLIOT O'DONNELL.

May 5, 1917.

4

CONTENTS

HAUNTED PLACES IN ENGLAND

CHAPTER I

THE CHAIR

THE CASE OF A HAUNTED HOUSE IN RED LION SQUARE

I AM not a psychometrist—at least not to any great extent. I cannot pick up a small object—say an old ring or coin—and straightway tell you its history, describing all the people and incidents with which it has been associated. Yet, occasionally, odd things are revealed to me through some strange ornament or piece of furniture.

The other day I went to see a friend, who was staying in a flat near Sloane Square, and I was much impressed by a chair that stood on the hearthrug near the fire. Now I am not a connoisseur of chairs ; I cannot always ascribe dates to them. I can, of course, tell whether they are oak or mahogany, Chippendale or Sheraton, but that is about all. It was not, however, the make or the shape of this chair that attracted me, it was the impression I had that something very uncanny was seated on it. My friend, noticing that I looked at it very intently, said : " I will tell you something very interesting about that chair. It came from a haunted house in Red Lion Square. I bought it at a sale there, and several people who have sat in it since have had very curious experiences. I won't tell you them till after you've tried it   Sit in it."

That wouldn't be any good," I answered ; " you know I can't psychometrise, especially to order. May I take it home with me for a few nights ? "

My friend smilingly assented.

The chair was put in a taxi, and in less than half an hour was safely lodged in my chambers. I was living alone just then, for my wife had been suddenly called away to the country, to the bedside of an aged and ailing relative. I say alône, but I had company—a lady tabby that, apparently abandoned by her lover, persisted in showering her attentions upon me. For hours at a time she would perch on the writing-table in my bedroom, whilst I was at work, and fix me amorously with her big green eyes.

The moment, however, this most eccentric of feline beauties perceived the chair, she sprang off her pedestal and dived under the bed ; and from that hour to this I have never seen her. The chair did not frighten me, but it brought a new, and I cannot say altogether pleasant, atmosphere into the place. When I was in bed and the gas was out, I could swear the chair moved, that it shifted nearer and nearer the window—always the window, as if it was most anxious to make its escape and hie back to its old home. And again there were times when, barred from this avenue of escape, it rocked. Yes, I could distinctly hear it rock backwards and forwards on the parquet floor with ever increasing rapidity and violence, as though blind with fury at being balked. And then, again, it groaned, groaned in the deepest and most hopeless misery—misery that the eternally damned alone can know and suffer. Certain now that there was something there that badly needed human consolation, I addressed the chair, and, failing to get any verbal answer from it, I tried a code of raps. That failing, I sat in it for several hours two successive nights, and experimented in automatic writing. The result was nil. Resolving to give it another trial, but this time without a planchette, I chose a Friday night when the moon was in the crescent, and placing the chair on one side the hearth, facing the window, I threw myself back in it and closed my eyes. For some minutes I was still vividly conscious of the old surroundings : the flickering fire flames — seen through my closed lids ; the old grandfather clock on the landing outside solemnly ticking ; the eternal whistling and hooting of the taxis as they whizzed along in the street beneath.

Then by degrees, quite imperceptibly, I lost cognisance of all these things ; and, intuitively, I began to feel the presence of something strange

and wholly novel in the room. I felt it steal
forth from a piece of dark and ancient tapestry
my wife had hung on the wall. It was merely a
shadow, an undefined shadow, a shadow such as
the moon, when very low in the heavens, might
possibly fashion from the figure of a man ; but
yet it was not a man, nor a woman, nor anything
with which I was in any way familiar. For a
moment it stood still, watching me from its vague,
formless, indefinite eyes. Then it made a forward
movement, stood still again, and yet once again
advanced.

Coming up behind my chair, it bent low over me,
and placing its long, cool spirit hands over my
eyelids, imparted to me a steadily increasing sense
of numbness. All thought was gradually annihil-
ated ; it was succeeded by a blank, just such a
blank as suddenly comes to one when in the hands
of the anæsthetist. Now, up to this evening, I had
presumed, as nearly everybody does presume, that,
in the case of mental blanks, every particle of consciousness is lost, totally arrested, and held, for
the time being, in complete subjection. But on
this occasion—at the very moment memory re-
asserted itself—I had recollections of some great
metempsychosis, some stupendous change in my
entire constitution, a change that affected all that
we term mind, and spirit, and soul.

I struggled earnestly and desperately to recall
the exact nature and process of that change, which
I now believe underlies all so-called blanks, and I
achieved this much : I recalled travel—a mad,

rushing plunge or descent into something—something quite different from anything I had known before—a descent into some plane, or sphere, or condition, wholly and completely apart from the physical, and what is generally understood and classified as the mental plane, sphere, or condition. In my efforts to recollect, I have arrived at that same pitch since ; but whenever I have been on the verge of getting beyond it, of forcing back a minute recollection of how that metempsychosis was enacted, of all the stages in it, there has been a lapse—my memory has dimmed. Yet brief and slight as these remembrances have been, they have assured me of one great truth, namely—that the state of blank never actually exists. Some part of us—the part that alone retains consciousness—is extracted and borne far away from the actual material body ; but on its return, on its reunion with the physical — with our gross and carnal, earthly self—all memory of this delicate and finely poised consciousness is at once swallowed up and obliterated. If such were not the case, if everything were indeed a blank, and the spiritual as well as the material part of us were suspended during what we term unconsciousness, we should be forced to the conclusion that the soul has no separate existence, that it cannot survive the body, and that the immortality of man, the infinite perpetuation of our identity, in which we have so fondly believed, is but a chimera. I am, however, certain—I could, if need be, swear to it—that even in the deepest slumber, in the wildest delirium, in the most seemingly omnipotent and annihilating blank, all is not lost, something remains, and that something is the psychic and spiritual consciousness, the very thing that constitutes what we term soul. In the first stage, then, of my cognisance of thought, again I struggled with memory, and the struggle overcoming me, I gradually lapsed into the mere consciousness of existence without thought. How long this condition lasted I cannot say, but with startling abruptness thought returned, and I became madly anxious to ascertain my present state—how it differed from my former —and my whereabouts. I was conscious of sound and light and motion, but conscious of them merely from the point of observation, as things quite outside myself—things that in no way sensibly affected me. What particularly impressed me was the silence—the passivity—of what, I believed, constituted my body. I could detect no heart movement, no pulsation whatever. I seemed to be there—to have a very familiar form—but to be nothing more than form—to have no tangibility. So far my eyes had seen ; but, purposely, I had not allowed myself to discriminate objects. I was intuitively certain my power of vision had become supernormal ; and I dreaded to employ it for fear I should see too much — too acutely. I had a stupendous sense of impending horror. At length, however, I was impelled by an irresistible fascination to look. I did so, and in an instant became the spectator of a drama. Before me, seated at a grimy wooden table, were two men, clad in the fascinating garb of· the latter part of the eighteenth century—long coat, befrilled vest, knee breeches, and peruke. Two mugs of ale were placed in front of them, and the one man kept on sipping, while the other, seldom touching the ale, took long and vigorous puffs at a pipe. The room had a very low ceiling, blackened with smoke, and traversed by enormous oaken beams ; a chimney corner, in which sat an old man, munching something out of a very dirty-looking bag, and, at the same time, taking occasional pinches of snuff ; and a couch, stowed away in one corner, and piled several feet high with a variety of books, papers, cushions, and wearing apparel.

The general atmosphere of the place suggested an inn or tavern. It was with the two men in the foreground, however, that something told me I was most concerned. They appeared to be about the same age and of the same class ; but there all similarity ended. The one was tall and thin, with dark, deep-set, and very restless eyes—and oddly noticeable hands. They were large and sinewy, with peculiarly long fingers and protruding knuckles. His companion was small and shrivelled, with watery blue eyes and a particularly weak mouth.

" Strange we should meet like this, John," the shorter of the two remarked, taking a big gulp of ale. " Ten years since we last saw one another, and that was in Bristol. Do you recollect the occasion ? "

" Do I recollect it ? " the other responded. " Can I ever forget it ? You had just come from her. She had accepted you. Money, of course. I had nothing to offer her but love. Love! What's the good of love without prospects?"

"It was a fair fight, John."

"Fair fight, Wilfred!" John replied. "You may call it fair, if you like, but I don't. What chance had I when you pointed to your bank-book and said, 'If I die I can settle all that on her'? I could promise nothing. I hadn't a cent in the world beyond my weekly pay. Thirty shillings. And how pleased you were with yourself when you came to see me that last evening in Bristol. Do you remember what you said? 'It's the fortune of war, my boy. You'll soon get over it. Work.' As if I didn't work! But I took your advice, though I hated you for it; and I left Bristol. After what had happened I loathed the place. An uncle of mine offered me a clerkship in his office in Holborn, and I stuck so hard to my job that I eventually became a partner."

"Then you're a rich man, John?"

"Comfortable, but not rich, Wilfred."

"And you've forgiven me? Got over that little love affair, eh? Well, well. Matrimony is not all bliss, John. At least that was my experience. Poor Jenny! But of course I have not told you. I'm much to be pitied, John."

"She's dead!"

"She is," Wilfred said, filling his mug with ale and raising it to his lips, "and I'm a lonely widower. But how did you know?"

"You wouldn't believe me if I told you," John

replied. " I get my information through channels that are barred to men like you."

" Witchcraft, I suppose," Wilfred said, with a sneer. " But why this mystery? Someone in Bristol city wrote to you."

" No, they didn't," John answered. " I know no one in Bristol city now. Your first suggestion was nearer the truth. Your wife, Wilfred, often comes to see me. I know all about the way in which you treated her."

" The way in which I treated her! " Wilfred cried, starting upright in his chair, his face flushing angrily. " God's truth, man, what do you mean by such a statement ? "

" I mean exactly what I say," John answered. " For the first two years you treated her tolerably well. Then someone else caught your fancy. Jenny was neglected, despised, and on one occasion actually beaten."

" It's a lie! " Wilfred gasped, springing to his feet, as if to leave the table.

" No, it's not," John retorted, " and you know it. Come, sit down, man, and go on drinking. Love never was in your line, drink is. Besides, as you say, she's dead, and what's the use of quarrelling over a corpse, even though she were beautiful as—as——" He didn't finish his sentence, but leaning forward thrust Wilfred back into his chair.

For some seconds the two men sat and looked at one another—Wilfred sullen, frightened, and resentful ; John imperturbable save for the perpetual restless movement of his eyes, and an occasional peculiar twitching of his upper lip and hands.

" A rum," John said at length, " or a gin? Or both ? "

" Rum."

" Very good, let it be rum." He called the waiter, and a rum was served.

" You're not drinking to-day, John," Wilfred remarked, taking a long pull at the rum and looking more amiable.

" No, I'm quite off spirits," John replied—" at least, spirits of that kind."

"Spirits of that kind ! " Wilfred sniggered. "Why, whatever other kind of spirits are there? What a mysterious fellow you are, John."

" Am I ? " John laughed. " Perhaps I've reason to be. I live in a big house, all alone, in Red Lion Square."

" New houses, aren't they ? " Wilfred commented. " And big rents? "

John nodded, the same nod answering apparently both questions.

" But you haven't told me yet," Wilfred went on, " how you knew Jenny was dead."

" I've seen her," John said very quietly. " She comes to me regularly."

"Seen her ? Comes to you regularly? You must be mad, John—mad or hoaxing. How can you see her, and why should she come to you ? "

John shrugged his shoulders.

" I told you you wouldn't believe me," he replied. " No one does. Yet I can swear to you it's true.

She appeared to me last night and told me you would be here this afternoon. That is how I happened to meet you."

" You overwork yourself, John," Wilfred said, taking another long pull at the rum. " Too much work is just as harmful to one's temperament and chances in life as too little. Moderation, my boy, moderation, I say. That's always been my keynote. I should like to see this house of yours."

" You shall," John said, " and the spirits. Not hers—I don't think you will see hers—but the rum and brandy. I've excellent brands of both—smuggled over from abroad last week."

" And yet you don't drink ! "

" No, I got them in entirely for your benefit. Come. We will go to my house. It's more comfortable than here. A big fire, nice easy chairs, tobacco, and bottles—bottles with plenty in them."

" And you've forgiven me, John ? "

" Forgiven you ! " John replied, rising from the table and putting on his hat. " Forgiven you! Do you think I should ask you round to my house, to drink the best vintage London can offer you, if I hadn't ? Come. Come along at once."

Wilfred rose with some difficulty from his seat, and the two men went out into the street. The scene then changed, and I found myself in a big, gloomy house, following them up a long flight of wooden stairs.

The moment I entered the house I became the victim of an anomalous species of fear. I saw nothing, but I instinctively knew that strange,

2

indefinable presences were there, watching us with sphinx-like faces.   I felt them, standing in the doorways, lurking in the angles of the hall and landings, and peering down at us from over the balustrades. I felt that they were merely critical at present, merely deliberating what attitude they should adopt towards us ; and I felt that the whole atmosphere of the house was impregnated with a sense of the utmost mystery—a mystery soluble only to those belonging, in the truest sense, to the spirit world—Neutrarians—spirit entities generated solely from spirit essence and never incarcerated in any material body—spirits initiated into one and all of the idiosyncrasies of spirit land.   The man John gave no outward signs of being in any way affected by these presences ; but it was otherwise with Wilfred.   The silence and darkness of the house unmistakably disturbed him, and as he panted up the staircase, following his long and lean host with none too steady a step, he cast continual looks of apprehension about him.   First, I saw him peer over his shoulders, down the stairs behind him, as if he fancied something, to which he could apply no name, might be treading softly at his heels ; then I watched his eyes wander nervously to the gloomy space overhead ; and then, as if drawn by some extremely unwelcome magnet, to the great, white, sinewy hands of John.   Arriving on the second floor, they crossed a broad landing and entered a spacious room, which was fitfully illuminated by a few dying embers in a large open grate. John produced a tinder box, lighted a trio of tall wax candles, and resuscitated the fire. He then left the room, reappearing in a few minutes with an armload of bottles.

"Make yourself comfortable, Wilfred," he said. "Take that easy chair and pull it up in front of the fire. Rum or brandy?"

Wilfred, whose eyes glittered at the sight of the spirits, chose rum. "I'll have a little brandy afterwards," he said, "just to wash down the rum. Moderation is my password, John, everything in moderation," and, helping himself to the rum, he laughed. John sat opposite him, and I noticed, not without some emotion, that the chair he took was the exact counterpart of the one in which I had left my material ego.

"John," Wilfred exclaimed after a while, "this house is most extraordinarily still. I—I don't like such stillness——" He was more than half drunk. "Why do you live alone? Damned silly habit to live alone in a house like this." Then he swallowed a big gulp of rum and leered.

"All habits are silly," John replied. "All life is silly. Death alone is sensible. Death's a fine thing."

Then there was a pause; and a gust of wind, blowing up the staircase, set the door jarring and made the windows rattle.

"I don't like that remark of yours, John," Wilfred suddenly stuttered. "Death's a fine thing?—Death's the work of the devil. It's the only thing I fear. And the—the wind. What's that?"

From the hall below there came a gentle slam, the soft closing of a door.

John shrugged his shoulders and stirred the logs until they gave out a big blaze.

"It's a noise," he said. "This house is full of noises. Every house is full of noises, if only you take the trouble to listen for them."

Another pause, and Wilfred helped himself to some brandy.

"Noises, like women," he said, "want keeping in their places. They've no business wandering about on nights like this. Hark!"

The faintest sound possible broke the stillness of the house; but it suggested much. To me it was like a light, bounding footfall on the first flight of stairs, those nearest the hall.

After listening a moment John spoke. "It's only Jenny," he said; "at least, I fancy it's only Jenny. But there are others. God alone knows whence they come or why. The house at times is full of them. So far I have only felt their presence—and heard. Pray to Heaven I may never see them—at least, not some. Do you hear that?"

There was a gentle rustling on the landing, a swishing, such as might have been caused by someone in a silk dress with a long train.

"It is—it's Jenny!" John went on. "I told you—she comes every night."

Wilfred made no reply, but the hand that held the glass shook so much that the brandy ran over and splashed on the floor.

There was again silence, then a creak, the

faint but very unmistakable turning of a door handle.

Wilfred's face blanched. He tried to look round, but dared not.

" I'm afraid too," John murmured, his teeth slightly chattering. " I never can get over my initial terror when she first arrives. God ! What horror I have known since I lived here."

The latch of the door gave a click, the sort of click it always gives when the door springs open, and a current of icy air blew across the room and fanned the cheeks of both men. Wilfred attempted to speak, but his voice died away in his throat. He glanced at the window. It was closed with heavy wooden shutters.

" It's no use," John sighed, " there's no escape that way. Make up your mind to face it—face HER. Ah ! " He sank back as he spoke and closed his eyes.

I looked at Wilfred. His vertebrae had totally collapsed ; he sat all huddled up in his chair, his weak, watery eyes bulging with terror, and the brandy trickling down his chin on to his cravat. All this scene, I must tell you, was to me most vivid, most acutely vivid, although I was but a passive participator in it. The same feeling that had possessed me on my entrance into the house was with me even in a greater measure now. I felt that pressing on the heels of this wind, this icy blast of air, were the things from the halls and landings, the distractingly enigmatical and ever-deliberating things. I felt them come crowding into the room ; felt them once again watching. Something now seemed to go wrong with the wicks of all three candles ; they burned very low, and the feeble, flickering light they emitted was of a peculiar bluish white. While I was engaged in pondering over this phenomenon my eye caught a sudden movement in the room, and I saw what looked like a cylindrical pillar of mist sweep across the floor and halt behind John. It remained standing at the back of his chair for a second or so, and then, retracing its way across the floor, disappeared through the door, which, opening wide to meet it, closed again with a loud bang. John opened his eyes and reaching forward poured himself out some brandy.

"I told you I didn't drink spirits," he said, "but her visit to-night has made a difference. Come, Wilfred, pull yourself together. The ghosts —at least her ghost has gone ; and as for the others, well, they don't count. Even you may get used to them in time. Come, come, be a man. For a sceptic, a confirmed sceptic, I never saw anyone so frightened."

Appealed to thus, Wilfred slowly straightened himself out, and peeping round furtively at the door, as if to make sure it really was shut, he helped himself to some more brandy. John leaned forward and regarded him earnestly. After some minutes Wilfred spoke.

"Those candles," he said, "why don't they burn properly ? I have never seen candles behave in that fashion before. John, I don't like this house."

John laughed. " Matter of taste and habit," he said. " I didn't like it at first, but I like it now."

Another pause, and then John said suddenly, " More brandy, Wilfred ? "

" No, I've had enough," Wilfred replied, " enough. John, I must be going home. See me to the door, John ; the front door, I mean, John. See me to the door, there's a good fellow." He tried to rise, but John put out one hand and pushed him gently back into his seat.

" It's early yet," John said, " far too early to go home. Think what a long time it is since we last met. Ten whole years. To some people almost a lifetime. Are you tired of life, Wilfred ? "

" Tired of life ? " Wilfred echoed. " Tired of brandy, perhaps, but not of life. What a question to ask ! Why ? " And again glancing furtively at the door he tried to rise.

Once more John put out his hand and thrust him back. " Not yet," he said ; " the hour is far too early. What were we talking about ? Being tired of life. Of course you are not. How foolish of me to ask you such a thing ! You who are so rich, respected, admired, beloved. You are happy in spite of your sad bereavement. You are a man to be missed. With me it is otherwise. I long to go to the spirit land, for it is there only I have friends, really genuine, loving friends. I am not afraid to die. I want death. I yearn for it. Yearn for it, Wilfred."

" Spirits ! Death ! Always spirits and death in your company," Wilfred responded. " Let's talk of something else—something more cheerful. I want cheering, John. This house of yours is depressing—most horribly depressing. You say it is new?"

"Comparatively new," John replied, and he started fumbling in his vest pocket.

"Comparatively new," Wilfred repeated, his eyes watching John's fingers attentively,—"and it has ghosts. Why, I thought it was only old houses that were haunted."

John chuckled. "So people say," he replied, "and they tell me I am mad to think there are ghosts here. They say it is impossible. What is your opinion, Wilfred?"

"Why," Wilfred said, watching John's movements with increasing interest, "that's my opinion too. A house to be haunted must have a history. And this house has none, has it? John!" The last syllable was uttered in an altogether different tone. It was not the voice of a drunken man.

For a brief moment John hesitated, trembled. He seemed to be in the throes of some great mental strain, some acute psychological crisis. But he speedily overcame it, and drawing his hand out suddenly from his vest, he produced a huge, murderous-looking clasp knife.

"True!" he said, "true. So far this house has no history. No history whatever. But it will have one, Wilfred. It will." And baring the blade of his formidable weapon, he crouched low and crept forward.

The next day I took the chair back to its owner. I had had enough of it—quite enough ; and I told him my experiences.

" Odd ! " he said, " very odd. The impressions you received when sitting in the chair are almost identical with those of the other people who have sat in it. I wonder if a murder did actually take place in that house ? I shouldn't be at all surprised. There is an old stain on the floor of one of the rooms on the second landing, and they say that, despite the most vigorous washing, it still retains its colour—red, blood-red."

CHAPTER II

THE HEAD

A DERBYSHIRE HAUNTING

SOME few years ago, two men were trudging along a road, not twenty miles from Sudbury, swearing heartily. It was not the first time they had sworn, not by any means, but it is extremely doubtful if either of them had ever sworn before quite so vehemently. There were, one must admit, extenuating circumstances. Having missed the last train, they were obliged to walk home, a distance of twelve or more miles, and having been overtaken by a rain-storm, they were soaked to the skin. True, the rain had now ceased, but as they had covered only six miles, they still had six more to go, and at every step they took, the water in their boots soaked through their socks and squished between their toes. Just as they arrived at a spot where the road swerved a little to their left and took a sudden dip, a clock from a distance solemnly chimed twelve.

The younger of the two men came to a halt and lighted his pipe. "Hold on a minute, Brown," he shouted; "I can't keep up this infernal pace any longer. Let's take an easy."

Brown turned and joined his companion, who

had seated himself on a wooden gate. Below them, in the dip, the darkness was sepulchral. The hedges on either side the road were of immense height ; and high above them rose the trunks of giant pines and larches, the intertwining branches of which formed an archway that completely obliterated the sky. A faint speck of light from afar flickered occasionally, as if through a gap in the foliage ; but, apart from this, the men could see nothing—nothing but blackness.

"A cheerful spot !" Brown remarked, "as gloomy a bit of road as I've ever seen. And how quiet !"

The other man blew his nose. " Not so quiet now," he laughed, "but how everything echoes ! What's that ? Water ? "

Both men looked, and, apparently, from the other side of the hedge, came the gentle gurgle of quick flowing water.

" Must be a spring," Brown observed, " flowing into some stream in the hollow. The darkness suggests the Styx. A match, if you please, Reynolds."

Reynolds gave him one, and for awhile the two men puffed away in silence.

Suddenly something whizzed overhead ; and they heard the prolonged, dismal hooting of an owl.

" This is getting a bit too eerie, even for my liking, Brown," Reynolds remarked ; " supposing we move on. I always associate noises like that with a death."

" I wish it were my mother-in-law's," Brown laughed, " or my own. But there's no such luck. I'm cold."

"So am I," Reynolds replied. "Deuced cold! Come on, do!"

He slid off the gate as he spoke and strode into the centre of the road.

The moon, temporarily unveiled, revealed as wet a landscape as one could possibly imagine. Everything dripped water—bushes, trees, ferns, grass, hats, clothes—whilst every rut of the road, every particle of soil, shone wet in the moon's rays. A deep, settled calm permeated the atmosphere. It was the stillness of night and moisture combined.

"What's the matter? Aren't you coming?" Brown asked impatiently.

"One moment," Reynolds replied. "I believe I heard footsteps. Hark! I thought so, they're coming this way! Someone else lost their train, perhaps."

Brown listened, and he, too, distinctly heard the sound of footsteps — high-heeled shoes walking along with a sharp, springy action, as if the road were absolutely hard and dry.

"A woman!" he ejaculated. "Odd hour for a woman to be out here."

Brown laughed. "Pooh!" he said. "Women are afraid of nothing nowadays except old age. Hullo! Here she comes!"

As he spoke the figure of a woman—slight and supple, and apparently young—shot into view, and came rapidly towards them.

Her dress, though quaint and pretty, was not particularly striking; but her feet, clad in patent leather shoes, with buckles that shone brightly in

the moonlight, were oddly conspicuous, in spite of
the fact that they were small and partially hidden
'neath a skirt which was long and frilled, and not at
all in accordance with the present fashion. Something about her prevented both men from speaking,
and they involuntarily moved nearer to one another
as she approached. On and on she came, tripping
along, and never varying her pace. Now in a zone
of moonlight, now in the dark belt of shadows
from the firs and larches, she drew nearer and
nearer. Through the hedge, Brown could dimly
perceive the figure of a cow, immensely magni-
fied, standing dumb and motionless, apparently
lost, like he was, in spellbound observation. The
silence kept on intensifying. Not a breath of air,
not a leaf stirring, not a sound from Reynolds,
who stood with arms folded like a statue; only
the subdued trickle, trickle of the spring, and the
hard tap, tap, tap of the flashing, sparkling shoes.
At last the woman was abreast of them. They
shrank back and back, pressing farther and farther
into the hedge, so close that the sharp twigs and
brambles scratched their faces and tore their
clothes. She passed. Down, down, down, still
tripping daintily, until the sepulchral blackness of
the dip swallowed her up. They could still hear
her tap, tap, tap; and for some seconds neither
spoke. Then Reynolds, releasing his clothes from
the thorns, muttered huskily : " At last I've seen
a ghost, and I always scoffed at them."
" But her head ! " Brown ejaculated, " where
was it ? "

"Don't ask me," Reynolds replied, his teeth chattering. "She had no head. At least I didn't see any. Dare you go on?"

"What, down there?" Brown said, nodding in the direction of the dip.

"Well, we must, if we are to get home to-night," Reynolds retorted, "and I'm frozen."

"Wait till that noise ceases, then," Brown answered. "I can't stand seeing a thing like that twice in one night."

They stood still and listened, until the tapping gradually died away in the far distance, and the only sound to be heard was that of the water, the eternal, never ceasing, never varying sound of the water. Then they ran—ran as they had never run since long ago Rugby days—down through the inky darkness of the hollow and out—far out into the brightness of the great stretch of flat country beyond; and, all the time they ran, they neither looked to the right nor to the left, but always on the ground just ahead of them.

.   .   .   .

For a week the horror of what they had seen was so great that neither of the two men could bear to be alone in the dark ; and they kept a light in their respective rooms all night. Then a strange thing happened. Brown became infatuated, he did nothing but rave, all day, about the ghost. She had the prettiest figure, the whitest hands, the daintiest feet he had ever seen, and he was sure her face must be equally lovely. Why couldn't he see it ? There was nothing about the neck to show she had been decapitated, and yet the head was missing. Why?

He worried Reynolds to death about it, and he gave no one else any peace. That waist, those delicate white fingers, those rosy, almond-shaped nails, those scintillating shoe buckles! They got on his brain. They obsessed him. He was like a maniac.

At last, at the suggestion of Reynolds, who wanted to get rid of him for awhile, he came up to London and paid visits to most of the professional mediums and occultists in the West End.

Some advised him one thing, and some another. Some immediately went into trances and learned from their controlling spirits all about the headless phantom, who she was, why she paraded the high road, and what had become of her head. But it was significant that no two told him alike, and that the head he so longed to see had at least a dozen different hiding-places. At last, when he had expended quite a small fortune, and his brain was much addled with psychic nomenclature, with detailed accounts of the Astral Plane, Karmas, Elementals, Elementaries, White Lodges, and What not, he interviewed a woman, living somewhere in the Bayswater direction, who suggested that he should hold a séance in the haunted hollow, and who promised, with a great show of condescension, to act as his medium if he would pay her the trifling sum of twenty pounds.

At first Brown declared the thing impossible, since he did not, at that moment, possess twenty pounds, which was literally true; but the prospect of seeing the ghost's face at length proved too much for him, and he decided to pawn all he had, in order to gratify his longing.

He closed with the offer. When the night fixed for the séance arrived, the weather conditions were all that could be desired ; the air was soft and calm, the moon brilliant, the sky almost cloudless, and promising only the finest weather for days to come. As the medium insisted upon a party of at least four, Brown persuaded a Mr. and Mrs. de Roscovi, Russians, to come, and they all set out together from Sudbury shortly after ten o'clock. Brown had made many inquiries in the neighbourhood as to the phantom figure, but he had only come across two people who would tell him anything about it. One, a farmer, assured him that he had on several occasions seen the ghost when driving, and that, on each occasion, it had kept abreast of his horse, even though the latter was careering along the road half mad with fright. But what terrified him most, he said, was that the apparition had no head.

The other, a blacksmith, said he had seen the woman twice, and that each time he had seen her she had been carrying something tucked under her arm, which he had fancied was a head. But he had been too scared to look at it very closely, and he only knew for certain that where her head should have been there was nothing. Both he and the farmer said they had heard all their lives that the road was haunted, but for what reason they had never been able to discover, as within the past sixty years, at any rate, neither murder nor suicide was known to have taken place near the hollow. This is as far as Brown had got with his investigations when he set out from Sudbury on the night in question. The de Roscovis did not think, for one moment, that the ghost would appear. They said, few people apparently had seen it ; its visits in all probability were only periodical ; and weeks, months, or even years might elapse before it put in an appearance there again.

" That may be, but then we have a medium," Brown argued. " I engaged her to invoke the ghost, provided it would not come of its own accord. You can invoke it, can't you, Madame Valenspin?"

Madame Valenspin now seemed rather dubious. " I have never tried in the open before," she said, with a slight shiver, " but I will do my best. The conditions seem favourable ; but I can't say definitely till we arrive at the exact spot."

Brown, however, could not help observing that the farther they advanced into the country, which became more and more lonely, the more restless and uneasy Madame Valenspin grew.

Once or twice she halted, as if irresolute whether to go on or not, and the moment she caught sight of the hollow she came to a dead stop.

" Not down there," she said. " It's too dark. We'd better stay here."

It was frightfully still. Brown listened for the murmuring of water. There was none. The recent hot sun had probably dried up the spring. Through the same gap in the hedge he saw a big cow— possibly, so he thought, the same cow—and he took it as a favourable augury for the appearance of the ghost that the animal, as before, was gazing fixedly into the open space, as if momentarily expecting to see something.

Behind it, away back in the broad expanse of field, were other cattle, their skins startlingly white; all motionless, and all in attitudes suggestive of a sense of anticipation, of a conscious waiting for something. The sepulchral hush was uninterrupted saving by bats, assuredly the biggest and blackest Brown had ever seen, wheeling and skimming, with the faintest perceptible whiz, whiz, whiz, in and out the larches; and the soft intermittent fanning of the leaves as the night breeze came rustling over the flat country and continued its career down into the hollow. A rabbit scurried across the road from one gate to another, its white breast shining silver, and some other small furry creature, of a species undetected, created a brief pandemonium in a neighbouring ditch. Otherwise all nature was extraordinarily passive.

" The figure went right down into the hollow," Brown said. " I think we ought to try there. What do you think, Mrs. de Roscovi ? "

" I am of the same opinion as Madame Valenspin," Mrs. de Roscovi replied, glancing apprehensively at the dip. "I think we had far better stay where we are."

" Very well, then," Brown said, " let's begin. You are mistress of ⸠the ceremonies, Madame Valenspin. Will you tell us what to do ? "

Madame Valenspin moved to one side of the road, and stood with her back resting against a gate. " Keep quite close to me," she said, " and I will try and go under control. Ah ! " She ejaculated the last syllable so sharply that Brown and Mrs. de Roscovi both started. She then began to mumble something, and then, breaking into a shrill, high-pitched key, stated that she was no longer Madame Valenspin but a spirit called Anne Heathcote, who was her temporary control. Anne Heathcote, so the audience were informed, was the ghost of a girl of very great beauty, who had been murdered in an adjoining field, close on a hundred years ago. There was no apparent motive for the deed, which was accomplished in a peculiarly barbarous fashion, the head being cut right off and thrown in a pit that had long since been filled in. The criminal was never caught.

" Can't you appear to us with your head on," Brown asked, " just as you were in your lifetime ? "

" No," the alleged spirit replied. " I am forbidden to do so. My visits are only periodical, and I shan't be able to materialise again here for at least ten years."

" Then there is little hope of my ever seeing you," Brown said, bitterly disappointed.

" None," was the somewhat abrupt answer.

" But why should you haunt this place at all ? " Mr. de Roscovi asked. " What reason is there for your being earth-bound ? "

" My sins," the control replied. " I was a very wicked girl."

" I don't care whether you were wicked or not," Brown put in mournfully. " I want to see you. If your face is in keeping with your limbs and figure, it must indeed be lovely. Is there no way of seeing you—just for a second ? "

" None," the control answered. Then, with much more emphasis, " None."

But hardly had the alleged Anne Heathcote spoken, when far away in the distance came the sound of footsteps. Tap, tap, tap !

"Why! By Jove!" Brown shouted, "there she is! I recognise her step. I should know it in a million."

For a minute everyone was silent, the tapping growing more and more audible. Then Madame Valenspin, in quite her own voice, exclaimed excitedly : " Let us be going. The spirits tell me we mustn't remain here any longer. Let's go back by the fields."

She fumbled with the latchet of the gate, against which she had been leaning, and hurriedly tried to raise it.

Mrs. de Roscovi said nothing, but gripped her husband by the arm. The steps approached rapidly, and presently the same dainty form, Brown had previously seen when with Reynolds, once more figured on the horizon.

" It is—it is she ! " Brown whispered. " Look —the waist, the arms, the hands, the shoes. Silver buckles ! How they flash ! "

An exclamation of horror interrupted him. It was from Mr. de Roscovi. He had moved to one side of the road, dragging his wife with him, and the two were standing huddled together, their eyes fixed in a frienzied stare at the phantom's neck. Brown, forcing his attention away from the long slim hands which so fascinated him, followed their glances. The neck was not as he remembered it, white and slender as far as it went, but it ended abruptly in a grey nothingness, and beyond this nothingness Brown fancied he discerned the dimmest of shadows. He was appalled but fascinated, and intense curiosity far outweighed his fear. He was certain she was beautiful—beautiful to a degree that immeasurably excelled any feminine loveliness he had hitherto encountered. He must see her face. He did not believe her head was missing ; he believed it was there on her body right enough, but that for some specific reason it had not materialised. He turned to Madame Valenspin to inquire the cause, and was greatly astonished to see her beating a hasty retreat across the fields. The figure had now come up to where he was standing, and tripping past him, it sped swiftly down the dip. Brown at once gave chase. He had not gone many yards before the darkness of the dip was on him ; and the only clue he had to his quarry's whereabouts was the sound of the shoes—the constant tap, tap, tapping. On and on he went, however, and at length, emerging from the darkness, he perceived a wooden stile and beyond it a tiny path, threading its way through a clump of firs that gradually grew thinner and thinner till they finally terminated in what appeared to be a broad clearing. Mounting the stile and springing off on the other side, the woman tripped along the path, and, turning for a moment to beckon Brown, disappeared from view,

The intense loneliness of the spot, emphasised a thousandfold by the eerie effect of the few straggling moonbeams that fell aslant the stile and pathway, and the knowledge that he had left his companions far behind made Brown falter, and it was some seconds before he could gather up the courage to continue his pursuit. A light girlish laugh, however, proceeding apparently from the spot where the figure had vanished, determined him. He saw once again vividly before him that willowy waist, those slim, delicate fingers, and those coquettish little feet. Were the devil itself to bar his way he must see her face. Sweating with terror, and yet withal obsessed with a passion that defies description, Brown mounted the stile and hastened in the direction of the laugh. Again it rang out, charged to overflowing with innocent fun and frolic, irresistibly girlish, irresistibly coy. This time there was no mistaking its locality. It came from behind a small clump of trees that bordered on the clearing. Wild with excitement and full of love madness, Brown dashed round the clump, and then halted. Floating in mid-air was a head, a head that looked as if it had long since been buried and just disinterred. The eyes alone lived, and they were fixed on Brown's with a mocking, baneful glitter. Hanging on either side of it was a mass of long fair hair, suggestive of a woman.

Every detail in the face stood out with hideous clearness in the brilliancy of the moonlight, and as Brown stared at it, petrified with horror, the thing laughed.

CHAPTER III

THE CUPBOARD

A CASE OF HAUNTINGS NEAR BIRMINGHAM

PEOPLE often wonder why new houses—houses without any apparent history—should suddenly begin to be haunted, often by a variety of very alarming phenomena, and then, just as suddenly, perhaps, cease to be haunted.

Of course one can only theorise, but I think a very possible and feasible reason is suggested, in the case I am about to relate.

Five years ago Sir George Cookham was living at " The Mayfields," a large country house some ten or twelve miles south-east of Birmingham. He · was greatly interested in criminology, inclining to the belief that crime is almost entirely due to physical malformation ; and used to invite all the great experts on the subject to stay with him. It was one week-end, towards the middle of September, that Dr. Sickertorft came ; and he and Sir George had some very heated arguments. Sir George was one of the most eccentric men I have ever met, and one of his many idiosyncrasies was to carry on his discussions walking.

On the morning of Sickertorft's departure he and

Sir George were arguing—Sir George, at the same
time, perambulating the corridor of the ground
floor of the house, for about the hundredth time—
when Dr. Sickertorft suddenly remarked : " I wonder
if this house is haunted ? "

" Haunted ! " Sir George laughed. " Why, of
course not. It's new. My father built it only
sixty years ago. A house to be haunted must be
old, must have some history. And the only tragedy
that has occurred here was when a servant I once
had, losing control of his temper, killed one of my
most valuable dogs. That was a tragedy, both for
the servant and the dog. There has been nothing
else to my knowledge—nothing beyond one or two
quite peaceful deaths from natural causes. But
why do you ask ? "

" Because," Sickertorft replied, " that cupboard
over there, opposite the foot of the stairs, to me,
strongly suggests a ghost. Something peculiarly
diabolical. Something that springs out on one
and imparts the sensation of being strangled."

" The only ghosts that haunt that cupboard,"
Sir George chuckled, " are boots and shoes, and, I
believe, my fishing rods. Ghosts are all a delusion—a peculiar state of the brain due to some
minute osseous depression or cerebral inflam-
mation."

" I don't agree with you," Sickertorft said
quietly. " I am positively certain that there are
such things as ghosts, that they are objective and
of many kinds. Some, in all probability, have
always existed, and have never inhabited any

human body ; some are the earth-bound spiritual egos of man and beast ; and some we can create ourselves."

" Create ghosts ! " Sir George cried. " Come, now, we are talking sense. Of course we can create ghosts. Pepper did, Maskelyne and Devant still do, and so do all the so-called materialising mediums."

" I don't mean spoof ghosts," Sickertorft responded. " I mean real ones. Real superphysical, objective phenomena. Man can at times create them, but only by intense concentration."

" You mean materialised thought forms ? "

" If you like to term them such," Sickertorft replied. " I believe they are responsible for a certain percentage of hauntings, but not all."

" Well, I've never seen any of your ghostly thought forms nor, in my opinion, am I ever likely to," Sir George growled. " Show me one and I'll believe. But you can't."

" I don't know so much," Sickertorft muttered, and, with his eyes still on the cupboard, he followed Sir George into his study.

.   .   .   .

A week later Lucy, a maid at " The Mayfields," was walking past the cupboard on her way to the dining-room, when something, as she subsequently described it to the cook, came over her, and she ran for her life.

" I didn't hear anything nor see anything," she explained. " I only felt there was something nasty hiding there, ready to spring out."

The following night she had the same experience, and her terror was so great that she ran shrieking into the dining-room, and it was some moments before she could make any coherent statement. Lady Cookham was very angry with her, and said it was all nonsense. There was nothing whatever wrong with the cupboard, and, if it occurred again, she must go. It did occur again, the very next night, and Lucy, without waiting for her dismissal, gave notice. She said this time she heard a laugh, a low chuckle, very sinister, and suggestive also of the utmost glee. The door of the cupboard creaked and, she believed, opened a little ; but on this point she could not be absolutely certain. She only knew her horror was infinitely greater than it had been on former occasions, and that when she ran, she was convinced something very dreadful ran after her.

The following evening, just about the same time, the butler went to the cupboard for a pair of shoes. He had just picked them up, and was about to go off with them, when someone breathed in his face. He sprang back in astonishment, striking his head somewhat badly against the edge of a shelf, whereupon there was a laugh—a short, sharp laugh, expressive of the keenest satisfaction. This was too much for the butler. Dropping the shoes, he dashed out of the cupboard and never ceased running till he was in the servants' quarters.

He told the housekeeper, and the housekeeper mentioned the matter to the head parlourmaid ; so that in a very short time the whole household got to know of it, and the cupboard was given as wide a berth as possible.

The next victim was the governess. Sir George had two children, both girls, and at present they were too young to go to school. The governess was a Cambridge graduate, who boasted of being utterly materialistic and of having a supreme contempt for weak nerves, and, to quote her own words, " poor simpletons who believe in ghosts."

She was passing the cupboard one evening, three nights after the butler's experience, when an irresistible impulse came over her to explore it. She opened the door and stepped inside, then someone closed the door with a bang and laughed.

" Who are you ? " the governess demanded. " Let me out at once. How dare you ! "

There was no reply, but when she stretched out her hand to feel for the door, she encountered something very cold and spongy, and the horror of it was so unexpected that she fainted.

In falling she struck the door violently. It flew open, and she was found some seconds later in a state of semi-insensibility, lying half in the cupboard and half across the corridor.

When Lady Cookham heard of what had happened, she was furious. " The cupboard can't be haunted," she declared, " it's ridiculous. Someone is playing us a trick. I'll call in the police."

The local inspector being summoned, examined the cupboard and cross-questioned the servants. But he discovered nothing. Lady Cookham now determined to unravel the mystery—if mystery there were—herself. She gave all the servants save one—the new maid Hemmings, whom she had engaged in the place of Lucy—a fortnight's holiday, and got in a supply cook from Coventry. The governess was allowed to remain, but she was strictly forbidden to go anywhere near the cupboard after midday.

When evening arrived, Lady Cookham, arming herself with a revolver and horsewhip, commenced to watch. Her first vigil passed uneventfully; but the next night, just as she had arrived at the cupboard and was taking up her stand facing it, the door slowly began to open. Lady Cookham is about as good a specimen of the thoroughly practical, strong-minded English sportswoman as one could meet anywhere. Up to the commencement of the present war she rode regularly with the Pytchley hounds, had a cold douche bath every morning, and spent a month at least every summer yachting in the English Channel.

She had never known fear—never, at least, until now. " Who's there ? " she demanded. " You had better speak sharp, or I'll fire ! "

There was no reply, however, and the door continued opening.

Had she seen anything, she doesn't think she would have been so frightened, but there was nothing—absolutely nothing visible. Her impressions were, however, that something was coming out, and that that something was nothing human.

It moved stealthily towards her—and she could define a soft clinging tread, just as if it had tentacles that kept adhering to the boards. She tried to press the trigger of the revolver, but her muscles refused to act, and when she opened her mouth to shout she could not articulate a sound. It was now close to her. One of its large, clammy feet touched her, and she could feel its clammy, pungent breath fanning the top of her head.

Then something icy cold and indescribably repulsive sought her throat and slowly began to throttle her. She tried to beat it off and to make some kind of noise to attract help, but it was all to no purpose. She was powerless. The grip tightened. All the blood in her veins congealed— her lungs expanded to the verge of bursting; and then, when the pain and horror reached its climax, and the identity of the hellish creature seemed about to reveal itself, there was a loud crack, and with it the acme of her sufferings, the final conscious stage of excruciating asphyxiation passed, and she relapsed into apparent death. She supposes that, for the first time in her life, she must have fainted. The crack was the report of her revolver. In her acute agony, her fingers had closed convulsively over the trigger, and the weapon had exploded.

The noise proved her salvation. No psychic phenomena can stand violent vibration, and Sir George Cookham, arriving on the scene at the sound of the report, found his wife lying on the ground unconscious, but alone. He heard her story, and refused to be convinced.

" It's a case of suggestion," he argued. " Lucy was a highly strung, imaginative girl. She had, in all

probability, been reading spook tales, and hearing
a noise in the cupboard had at once attributed the
sound to ghosts. That was quite enough for
Wilkins. Servants are ready to believe anything
—especially if it is propagated by one of their
own class. Miss Dennis is a hypochondriac. All
governesses must be. The nature of their work
necessitates it. She heard a well-garnished account
of what was supposed to have happened from
Wilkins, probably from Lucy too, and the neurotic
state of her nerves did the rest. Of course when
it comes to you, my dear," he said, "it is more
difficult to understand. But as there are no such
things as ghosts—as they are a scientific impossibility—it must have been suggestion."

"I'm certain it was not," Lady Cookham retorted, "and I'm going to leave the house and take
the children with me. It's not right for them to
stay."

Sir George protested, but Lady Cookham had
her own way, and in less than a fortnight there
were notices in the *Field*, and other papers, to say
that "The Mayfields" was to be let furnished.

"We'll give it a year's trial," Lady Cookham
said, "and, if the people who take it are not disturbed by anything unusual happening, we will
conclude the hauntings are at an end and return."

A few days after this conversation Sir George
met Dr. Sickertorft on the platform of Coventry
Station. Though the day was almost sultry, the
doctor was muffled up in an overcoat, and appeared
very pale and thin.

" So you are leaving ' The Mayfields,' " Sickertorft remarked. " Has the ghost been too much
for you ? "

" Ghost ! " Sir George cried angrily, " what the
deuce do you mean ? We have let the house for
awhile, but not on account of any ghost. My wife
wants to be nearer London."

" Then the stories that have got afloat are
all moonshine," Sickertorft replied, with a
smile, " and you are still just as sceptical as
ever."

" I am," Sir George responded ; " and if you hear
any more reports about ' The Mayfields ' being
haunted, kindly contradict them."

Sickertorft smiled. " I will make a bet, Sir
George," he said, " that you will be converted one
day."

" You may bet as much as you like, but you'll
lose," Sir George answered furiously. And turning
his back on Sickertorft, he walked away from him
without another word.

The following day Lady Cookham and the
children left, and Sir George finding himself the
sole occupant of the house, the servants having left
at midday, telephoned to Sydney N. Morgan, a
well-known private detective who specialised in
cases of theft and blackmail, asking him to come.
On his arrival at " The Mayfields " that same
evening, Morgan listened to all Sir George had to
say, and then made an exhaustive examination
of the premises, paying particular attention to the
cupboard in the hall.

" Well ? " Sir George asked. " What is your opinion ? Rats ? "

" Not human ones, at any rate," Morgan replied. " Anyhow, I can find no traces of them. I incline to your theory of nerves."

" Imagination first and then suggestion." Sir George grunted. Now that he was alone there with the detective, he began to have misgivings. The house seemed strangely large and silent. But ghosts ! Bah ! There were no such things. He said as much to Morgan, and they both laughed.

Then they stared at one another in amazement, for, from afar off, there came an answering echo, a faint yet distinctly audible—chuckle.

They were standing at one end of the corridor on the ground floor when this happened, and to both of them the sound seemed to emanate from the cupboard. " What was that ? " Sir George asked. " The wind ? "

" It may have been," Morgan said dubiously, " but there's no getting away from the fact that it was a queer noise for the wind to make. I made sure I looked everywhere."

" I'll go upstairs and get my revolver," Sir George observed. " It may come in handy. Will you remain here ? "

They looked at one another furtively, and each thought they saw fear in the other's eyes.

Both, however, had reputations to sustain.

" I'll wait down here, Sir George," Morgan said, " and keep an eye on the cupboard. You'll call if you want me."

" I will," Sir George replied. " I shan't be gone more than a minute. Be on your guard. It's just about this time the alleged disturbances begin."

He hurried off, and Morgan watched his long legs cross the hall and hastily ascend the main staircase. The hall occupied a large space in the centre of the house, and overlooking it was a gallery connecting the east and west wings.

Sir George's room—that is to say, the room he was reserving for himself on this occasion—was in the east wing, the first to be reached from the gallery, and Morgan could almost see it from where he stood in the hall. His gaze was still fixed on Sir George's retreating figure when a noise from behind him made him turn hurriedly round, and he distinctly saw the cupboard door open a few inches. Moving towards the cupboard, he then saw, as the door opened wider, a huge indefinable something emerge from it. Morgan admits that the most sublime terror seized him, and that he shrank back convulsively against the wall, totally unable to do anything but stare. The shape came towards him with a slow, shambling gait, and Morgan was at length able to compare it with an enormous fungus. It had arms and legs truly, but they were disproportionately long and crooked, and hardly seemed to belong to the body.

There was no apparent head. The whole thing was vague and misty, but suggestive of the greatest foulness and antagonism. Morgan's horror was so great as it passed him that he believes his heart practically stopped beating, and so tightly had he clenched his hands that the print of his finger nails remained on his palms for days afterwards. It left him in time, however, and he watched it shuffle its unwholesome way across the hall and surreptitiously begin to ascend the staircase.

He tried to shout to Sir George to put him on his guard, but his voice refused to act and he could do nothing.

Up and up it went, until at last it reached the gallery and crept onward into the east wing.

He then heard Sir George cry out, "Hullo, Morgan! Is that you? Anything——" There was then a moment of the most intense silence, and then a shriek. Morgan says it was like a woman's shriek—it was so shrill, so uncontrolled, so full of the most abject terror. For a moment it completely paralysed Morgan, but he seems then to have partially recovered. Anyhow, he pulled himself sufficiently together to run up the stairs and arrive outside Sir George's door in time to hear sounds of a most violent struggle. Tables, chairs, washstand, crockery, were all hurled to the ground, as Sir George raced round and round the room in his desperate efforts to escape. Once he caught hold of the handle of the door and turned it furiously. "Let me out!" he shrieked. "For mercy's sake let me out!" and again Morgan heard him rush to the window and pound madly on the glass.

Then there came another spell of silence—short and emphatic—then a shriek that far eclipsed anything Morgan had hitherto heard, and then a voice—a man's voice, but certainly not Sir George's

—which, speaking in sharp, jerky sentences that conveyed with them a sense of strange far-offness, said : " You'll believe now, Sir George. You'll believe now. Damn you, you'll believe now ! " Then there were sounds as if someone was being shaken very violently to and fro, and Morgan, utterly unable to stand it any longer, turned tail and—fled.

.   .   .   .

When Morgan returned some half an hour later, accompanied by the lodge-keeper and one of the under-gardeners, they found Sir George lying in a heap on the floor—unconscious. He did not die, however, neither did he go mad ; but his heart was badly affected, and he subsequently developed fits.

Nothing would induce him to describe what had actually taken place, and this, added to the fact that he never again set foot within " The Mayfields," caused his friends to draw their own conclusions. Morgan told me all about it, and I at once wrote to Dr. Sickertorft. I was too late, however ; Dr. Sickertorft had been dead some weeks—he had died of cerebral tuberculosis exactly three months after Morgan's visit to " The Mayfields." I was informed that he attributed the fatal malady to supernormal concentration.

CHAPTER IV

THE EMPTY· LEASH

A CASE OF HAUNTING IN ST. JOHN'S WOOD

I HAVE so often been accused of writing too exclusively about the horrid types of spirit, such as earth-bound murderers, suicides, and elements, that I am more than pleased to be able to present to my readers a case of a different kind. Until quite recently Barcombe House, St. John's Wood, was haunted by the ghost of a very lovely little girl, who, it is believed, died of a broken heart because a dog to which she was very much attached had to be destroyed. I obtained particulars as to the hauntings from a Mr. John Tyley, whose verbatim account I will endeavour, as nearly as possible, to reproduce.

"Guy Darnton is a very intimate friend of mine. Some people call us inseparables, and I suppose we are—though at times, I believe, no two men could so thoroughly hate one another. Indeed, to such an extremity has this spirit of execration and dislike been carried that I have on occasions actually accused him of being my very worst—my most cruel, and certainly my most subtly destructive— enemy. But even then, even at the moment when my abhorrence of him has been most acute, I have always accorded him—reluctantly, I admit—one great redeeming quality—his affection for and kindness to Ghoul.

" Ghoul was an Irish terrier, just an ordinary-looking Irish terrier, with all the pugnacious and—as some unkind critics would add—quarrelsome characteristics of his race. He' hated fops, those little brown Pekinese and King Charles horrors that ladies scent and comb, and stuff to bursting-point with every imaginable dainty; and whenever he saw one mincing its way along the street, he would always block its path and try to bite it.

" Yet he was an idealist. It's all nonsense to say that animals have no appreciation of beauty. Ghoul had. He was fond of biscuits truly; but he liked other things more, far more than food. I have known him stand in front of a rose bush and gaze at it with an expression which no one but the most unkind and prejudiced sceptic could possibly misinterpret for anything but sheer, solid admiration ; and I used to notice that whenever he was introduced to several ladies, he always wagged his tail hardest at the prettiest of them. But most of all Ghoul admired pretty children—dainty little girls with fluffy yellow curls and big, smiling eyes. He adored them, and he hated with equal fervour all children who were in any way physically ill-favoured. I have known him bark furiously at a boy who squinted, and snarl at and refuse to go near a girl who had a blotchy, yellow complexion and a cavernous, frog-shaped mouth.

" But I am speaking as if Ghoul were my property. He was not—at least, not in the legal sense. Darnton paid for his licence—and housed and fed him—and so had every apparent right to call himself Ghoul's master.

" In spite of this, however, I knew intuitively that Ghoul regarded me as his actual master, and I believe the explanation of this circumstance lay in the superphysical. I am psychic, and I am convinced that the unknown is nearer, far nearer to me than it is to most people. Now dogs, at least most dogs, have the faculty of second sight, of clairvoyance and clairaudience, very acutely developed—you have only to be in a haunted house with them to see it ; and there is nothing they stand in awe of more—or for which they have a more profound respect—than the superphysical. Now Ghoul was no exception. He saw around me what I only felt ; and he recognised that I was the magnet. He respected me as one true psychic respects another.

" One day we were out together. Darnton had gone to the dentist, and Ghoul, tired of his own company, resolved to pay me a visit. He wandered in at the wicket gate of my garden just as I was about to set off for a morning constitutional. I greeted him somewhat boisterously, for Ghoul, when extra solemn, always excited my risibility, and, after a brief skirmish with him on behalf of my cat, an extraordinarily ugly Tom, for whom Ghoul cherished the most inveterate hatred, we set off together. It was pure accident that led me into the Adelaide

Road. I was half-way along it, thinking of nothing in particular, when someone whistled behind me, and I turned round. As a rule, one may see a few pedestrians—one or two at least—at all times of the day in the Adelaide Road, but oddly enough no one was in sight just at that moment, and I could see no traces of Ghoul. I called him, and getting no reply, walked back a little distance. At last I discovered him. He was in the front garden of Barcombe House, sitting in the centre of a grass plot, his eyes fixed on space, but with such an expression of absorbing interest that I was absolutely astounded. Thinking something, perhaps, was hiding in the bushes, I threw stones and made a great shooing ; but nothing came out, and Ghoul still maintained his position. The look in his .face did not suggest anything antagonistic, it was indicative rather of something very pleasing to him— something idealistic—something he adored.

" I shouted ' Ghoul ! ' He did not take the slightest notice, and when I caught him by the scruff of the neck, he dug his paws in the ground and whined piteously. Then I grew alarmed. He must either have hurt himself or have gone mad. I examined him carefully, and nothing appearing to be the matter with him, I lifted him up, and, despite his frantic struggles, carried him out of the garden.

" The moment I set him down he raced back. Then I grew determined. A taxi was hailed, and Ghoul, driven off in it, speedily found himself a close prisoner in Darnton's exceedingly unromantic study.

"That afternoon I revisited Barcombe House alone. The premises were to let, and, judging by their neglected and dilapidated appearance, had been so for some considerable time. Both front and back garden were overgrown with a wild profusion of convolvulus, thistles, and other weeds; and an air of desolation, common to all abandoned houses, hung about the place. All the same, I could detect nothing unpleasant.

"I was unmistakably aware of some super-physical influence; but that influence, unlike the majority of those I had hitherto experienced, was decidedly attractive.

"It seemed to affect everything—the ruddy rays of sunlight that, falling aslant the paths, turned them into scintillating gold; the buttercups and dandelions more glorious yellow than I had ever remembered seeing them; the air—charged to overflowing with the rich, entrancing perfume of an abnormally generous summer's choicest flowers. All nature here seemed stimulated, cheered and glorified, and the longer I lingered the longer I wished to linger. At the far end of the garden was an arbour overgrown with jasmine and sweet honeysuckle, and on its moss-covered seat I espied a monstrous Teddy bear adorned with a piece of faded and mildewy pink ribbon. The sight filled me with a strange melancholy. The poor Teddy bear, once held so lovingly in the tight embrace of two little infantile arms, was now abandoned to the mercies of spiders and wood-lice, and the pitiless spoliation of decay. How long had it been left, and where was its owner? I looked at the sunshine, and, in the beams that gilded every-thing around me, I felt an answer to my queries. Most haunted places scare me, but it was otherwise here ; and I was so fascinated, so eager to probe the mystery to its core, that I left the garden and, crossing a tiny stone yard, approached the back of the house. The premises were quite easy of access, as the catch of one of the windows was broken, and the shutter of the coal-house had come off its hinges. One has always supposed that the basement of any house that has stood empty for a long time must become cold and musty, but here I could detect neither cold nor mustiness. Even in the darkest recesses the sun made its influence felt, and its beams warmed and illuminated walls and flagstones alike. I now entered a large and lofty apartment, with a daintily tiled floor, spotlessly clean ceiling, artistically coloured walls, and scrupulously clean dresser. Here again the devastating hand of decay was nowhere to be seen, and indeed I thought I had never been in such a pleasant kitchen.

" I intended waiting there only until I had con-sumed a sandwich, but when I rose to go, some-thing held me back, and I tarried on and on, until the evening set in and dark and strangely formed shadows began to dim the walls and floor.

" As I was mounting the stairs to explore the upper premises a gentle gust of wind blew in my face and filled my nostrils with the most delightful odour of ' cherry-pie.' Intoxicated, I halted, and, leaning against the banisters, inhaled the perfume

to the full extent of my lungs. Then I listened.
The breeze rustling past me down the stairs rattled
the window panes and jarred the doors, and seemed
to disseminate, in its wake, new and even more per-
plexing shadows. Presently a door slammed, and
I distinctly heard footsteps cross the hall and begin
to ascend the stairs.

" It was now for the first time that terror laid
hold of me, but the fascination of it was so com-
pelling that I lowered my head over the balustrade
to listen. I tried to reason the thing out. Why, I
asked myself, should these footsteps alarm me ?
What was it that made them different from other
footsteps ? Surely there was no difference. And
yet, if that were so, why was I certain that they
were not the footsteps of any trespasser from outside ? I debated earnestly, desperately, but could
arrive at no other conclusion than that there was a
difference, and that this difference did not lie in
the sounds themselves, but in the sense of atmosphere they conveyed, an atmosphere that was
peculiarly subtle and quite incompatible with the
natural. At last I knew for certain that the sounds
were superphysical, and yet such was my dread
of the Unknown that I fought most frantically
against my convictions.

" The steps had, by this time, so I calculated,
reached the first landing, and I now noticed in
them a cautiousness that I had not remarked
before. What should I see ? There was still
time for flight, but whither could I go ? Behind
me were a row of half-open doors, through which

the sun, sinking fast, shone its last rays. The effect—a sad one—forcibly reminded me of the end of all`things—death ; and the sadness of it harmonised well with an air of silent expectation that seemed suddenly to have filled the whole house. My fears grew. I was certain that the oncoming footsteps could only emanate from a phantom of the most startling and terrifying description, and I bitterly repented of my rashness in coming to the house alone. With a supreme effort, I averted my gaze and turned to seek refuge in one mad headlong plunge, should there be no other haven, through a window ; but the power to do so was denied me. I was paralysed. The steps came nearer, and now, some distance below me, moving rapidly up the staircase, came something bright. I watched it pass swiftly round one bend, and then another, and at the moment my suspense had reached its limit and I felt I was on the border-line of either death or insanity, it turned the last corner and shot fully into view. The reaction was then so great that I reeled back against the wall and burst out laughing. Instead of some distorted semblance of humanity, instead of some grotesque, semi-animal elemental, something too grim and devilish for the mind to conceive and survive, I saw—a child : a girl of about twelve, dressed in the most becoming frock of soft white satin, high in the waist, and from thence falling in folds to her feet. She had long bright golden hair hanging in loose curls on either side of her low white forehead ; delicately pencilled eyebrows that were slightly knit, and wide open blue-grey eyes that were fixed on me with an expression of the gravest anxiety, mingled with a something enigmatical, something sorely puzzling and with which I seemed to be familiar. Again and again I have tried to diagnose it, and at times the solution has seemed very near ; but it has always eluded me in the end, and the mystery is still as great and as poignant as ever. The child held a leash in one hand, whilst she stretched out the other confidingly towards me.

" Always a worshipper of beauty, I was stooping down to kiss her little hand, when, to my consternation, she abruptly vanished, and I found myself standing there—alone.

" An intense sadness now seized me, and throwing myself on the floor I gave way to an attack of utter dejection. The vision I had just seen was in very deed the embodiment of all my boyhood's dreams, and for the moment, but only for the moment, my old self, a little pensive boy adoring heart and soul a girl's fair face, had lived again.

" It was all too cruelly brief ; for with the vision my old ego vanished too ; and I felt—I knew it had been wrested from me and hurried to some far-off place where the like of my present self could not be admitted. I rose at length chilled and hopeless, and tearing myself away from the landing with a desperate effort, wandered home. I could not rest. An intense dissatisfaction with myself, with my whole mode of life, my surroundings, obsessed me. I longed to alter, to become something different, something unsophisticated, simple, even elementary. This change in me brought me into closer sympathy with Ghoul, who, as I have said, was strangely altered himself. He avoided Darnton with the most marked persistence, and was always hovering round my doorstep and lying on the lawn. At last one day I could stand it no longer. ' Ghoul,' I said, ' the same yearning possesses us both. It's the child—the child with the lovely eyes. We must see her. You and I are rivals, old fellow. But never mind ! We'll visit the house together and let her take her choice. Come along ! '

" Ghoul's joy on entering the garden of Barcombe House knew no bounds. He tore in at the gate, capered across the grass, barked, whined, wagged his tail furiously, and behaved like the veriest of lunatics. Gaining admittance into the house as easily as before, I quickly made my way to the third-floor landing, Ghoul darting up the stairs ahead of me. Without a moment's pause he bolted into a room immediately in front of us, and springing on to the sill of a large casement window that was wide open, peered eagerly out, exhibiting, as he did so, the wildest manifestation of excitement. Following the direction of his eyes, I looked down into the garden, and there, gazing up at us, her curls shining gold in the hot summer sun, stood the little ghost. The moment she saw me, she smiled, and, moving forward with a peculiar gliding motion, entered the house. Once again a door slammed, and, once again, there came the patter of ascending footsteps. Ghoul ran to meet her.

She stooped over him, patted his head and fastened the leash to his collar, whilst I, merely a spectator, felt the bitterest pangs of jealousy. Then she looked up, and instantly the joy in her face was converted into pity—pity for me. Without a doubt Ghoul had triumphed.

" Still patting him on the head and urging him forward, she ran past me, and, mounting the window sill, glanced round at me with a mischievous smile. Even then I did not comprehend the full significance of her action. I merely stood and stared— stared as if I would never grow tired of staring, so fascinated was I by the piquante beauty of that superhuman little face. I was still staring when she put one foot through the open window ; still staring when the other foot followed ; still staring when she waved her hand gleefully at me and sprang out—out into the sunny brightness of the hot summer noon. I thought of Ghoul. He had sprung, too. Sprung barking and whining with a joy unequalled.

" I ran to look for him. He lay where he had fallen, his neck broken and his spirit fled.

" Darnton, of course, would not believe me. We had a stormy interview, and we have never spoken to one another since.

" The house—Barcombe House—is now let, and the occupants inform me that they have never once been troubled—at least not by ghosts."

CHAPTER V

THE DRESSING-ROOM

CASES OF HAUNTINGS AT THE PRINCE REGENT AND OTHER THEATRES

THE idea of a theatre being haunted—a theatre where everything is bright and everyone full of life—must, for the moment, strike one as preposterous. Why, the mere thought of the footlights, to say nothing of the clapping of hands and thunders of applause from the Gods, conjures up a picture which is the very antithesis of ghosts. Besides, why should a theatre be haunted ? To be haunted, a place must have a history—someone must have committed a crime there, such as murder or suicide ; and surely no such thing has ever happened in a theatre ! Imagine a murder, a real one, at Drury Lane, or a suicide, say, at the Gaiety ! Why, the thing is monstrous, absurd ! And as to a ghost—a *bona fide* ghost—appearing on the stage or in the auditorium, why, such an idea is without rhyme or reason ; it is, in fact, inconceivable,' and the public—the all-wise public—would, of course, laugh it to scorn.

But stop a moment. Does the general public know everything ? Is not the theatre, to it, simply

the stage, and is it not profoundly ignorant of all
that lies beyond the stage—away back, behind the
hidden wings? Is it not profoundly ignorant,
also, of the great basement below the stage with its
dark and tortuous passages; and profoundly
ignorant of the many flights of cold and carpetless
stairs, leading to story upon story of seemingly
never-ending dressing-rooms and corridors? What
does it know, too, of the individual lives of the
many generations of actors and actresses, call-
boys and dressers who have toiled wearily up those
stairs and along those dimly lit passages in between
the acts? what does it know of the thoughts of all
that host of bygones—of their terrible anxieties,
their loves, their passions? what does it know of
the tragedies with which, doubtless, many of these
people have been intimately associated, and of the
crowd of ghosts they have, wittingly or unwittingly,
brought with them from their own homes?—for
ghosts, even as they haunt houses, haunt people
and mercilessly attach themselves to them. Moreover, although they have long since been forgotten,
tragedies have occurred in some of the oldest of the
London theatres. Hunt up the records of eighty
and ninety years ago, and you will find that more
than one dressing-room witnessed the tragic ending
of some lesser star, some member of the crowd, a
mere " walker on " ; that duels were not infrequently
fought in grim earnest on the boards ; and that more
than one poor super has been found hanging from
a cobwebby beam in a remote corner of the great
maze-like basement of the building.

Again, think of the site of a London theatre ! Prehistoric man or beast may well lie buried there ; witches accused of practising their nefarious rites on or near that site may well have been burnt there. Think, too, of the houses that once may have stood there ! Inns, with dark tell-tale stains on their boards ; taverns, tainted with vice—the rendezvous of truculent swashbucklers and painted jades ; and even more terrible still, cruel and ghastly slaughter-houses.

Ground, then, and houses alike, all may have had their hauntings ; and the ghosts may have stayed on, as ghosts often do, haunting anew each successive building. Yes, more than one London theatre is haunted—and several of these theatres have more than one ghost.

The proprietors affect ignorance and of course tell you nothing. They like to see long queues of people waiting for admission to their show, but they have no desire to see a corresponding crowd at the box office seeking permission to sit up all night in the theatre to see the ghost. No, if you want to find out if a theatre is haunted, you must not apply to the proprietor, you must inquire of the actors themselves ; and, in order to stand a really good chance of discovering the truth, you should, if possible, for a time become one of them. It was for the purpose of making such a discovery that I took it into my head one day last year to apply for a walk on at the Mercury. I had often wondered if the Mercury was haunted. I speedily found out that it was not. Still, I was not altogether disappointed, for I learned from some of my fellow-walkers on and from one of the stage hands of several very interesting cases of hauntings at other of the London theatres. There is the Prince Regent's, for instance, which, as recently as the late nineties had a dressing-room, 25, that was always kept locked. It was in the autumn of 1897 that John W. Mayhewe was engaged to play a small but rather important part there in *The Merciful Pirate*. The cast was an unusually large one, and Mayhewe discovered that he had to share dressing-room 25 with another actor called Talbotson. The opening night of the play, however, Talbotson was laid up with influenza, and Mayhewe had room 25 to himself. Being one of those over-anxious people who err on the side of being ultra-punctual, he arrived at the theatre at least an hour before the curtain went up, and, on the way to his room, he paused to chat with the stage doorkeeper.

" I noticed," he remarked, " when I was dressing for rehearsal yesterday that my room smelt very musty. Isn't it often used ? "

" It hasn't been used since I've been here," was the reply.

" Why ? " said Mayhewe.

" I can't tell you," the doorkeeper answered surlily. " If you want to know, you had better ask the stage manager."

Not caring to do this, Mayhewe made no further remarks, but hastened upstairs. No one was about, and the noise of his footsteps sounded strangely loud in the silent emptiness of the passages. He entered his room at last, hung his coat and hat on the door, and, crossing to his seat in front of a small mirror, sat down. " After all," he said to himself, " I'm glad Talbotson won't be here to-night. I'm not in a mood for talking, and the fellow bores me to distraction." He lit a cigarette, leaned back in a more comfortable attitude, and for some minutes allowed himself to revel in the luxury of a perfectly blank state of mind. Suddenly the handle of the door turned—a solitary, isolated sound—and he sat up sharply in his chair. " Who's there ? " he shouted. There was no response. " I couldn't have latched it properly," he reasoned, and once again he leaned back in his chair and smoked. Five or six minutes passed in this fashion, and he was thinking of beginning to dress, when there was another noise. Something behind him fell on the floor with a loud flop.

Once again he turned swiftly round. It was his hat—a hard felt bowler. It had fallen from the door peg on which he had hung it, and was still feebly oscillating.

" It is curious how one sometimes notices all these little things," he reflected. " I dare say door handles have turned and hats have fallen a thousand times when I might have heard them and haven't. I suppose it is because everything is so very quiet and I'm alone in this part of the building." Then he glanced at his coat—a long, double-breasted ulster — and rubbed his eyes thoughtfully. " Why," he exclaimed, " what a curious shape the thing has taken! It's swelled out just as if someone were inside it. Or has my eyesight suddenly gone wrong?" He leaned forward and examined it closely. No. He was not mistaken. The coat was no longer untenanted. There was something inside it—something which filled it like he had done; but it was something to which he could ascribe no name. He could see it there, and mentally feel that it was peering at him with eyes full of the most jibing mockery and hate; but he could not define it. It was something quite outside his ken, something with which he had had no previous acquaintance. He tried to whistle and appear nonchalant, but it was of no avail. The coat—his coat—had something in it, and that something was staring back at him. What a fool he had been to come so early. At last, with a supreme effort, he took his eyes from the door, and, swinging round in his chair, resumed smoking. He sat thus for some moments, and then a board close behind him creaked.

Of course there is nothing in a creak—boards and furniture are always creaking, and most people attribute the creaking to a change in the temperature. So did Mayhewe. "The room is beginning to get warm—the gas has heated it," he said; "that is why." Still he gradually lowered his eyes, and when they rested on the mirror in front of him, he gave the barest suspicion of a start. In the mirror were reflected the door and the coat, but the latter hung quite limply now. There was nothing whatever filling it out.

What in Heaven's name had become of the thing?

Where had it got to ? Close beside Mayhewe was the grate, and a sudden rustling in it, followed by a hurried descent of soot, made him laugh outright. The explanation was now so very simple. The wind was responsible for it all—for the door handle, the hat, the coat, and the creak. How truly ridiculous! He would dress. With that object in view he threw the end of his cigarette in the fender ánd, rising, was about to quit his seat, when his eyes fell on his gloves. He had thrown them quite carelessly on the wash-stand, almost immediately in front of him, and he had noticed nothing remarkable about them then. But now —surely it could not be the wind this time ; there were hands in them, and these hands were strangely unlike his own. Whereas his fingers had blunt, spatulate tips, the tops of these fingers were curved and pointed like the talons of some cruel beast of prey, and the palms were much longer and narrower than his own. He stared at them, too fascinated to do otherwise, and it seemed to him that they shifted their position and came nearer to him, with a slow, stealthy, silent motion, like that of some monstrous spider creeping murderously towards its helpless victim. He watched them for some moments quite motionless, and then, yielding to a sudden fit of ungovernable fury, he threw his tobacco pouch at the nearest.

It rolled convulsively over on its back after the manner of some living stricken creature, and then, gradually reassuming its shape, stealthily began once more to approach him. At last his nerves could stand it no longer. A demoniacal passion to smash, burn, torture it seized him, and, springing to his feet, he picked up his chair, and, swinging it round his head, brought it down with the utmost frenzy on the wash-stand. He was looking at his handiwork—the broken china, chair legs, and gas shade—when the door of his room opened and the call-boy timidly entered.

Mayhewe kept the stage waiting some minutes that night, but the management did not abuse him nearly so violently as he had anticipated, and the next evening he was allotted another room.

Then it transpired, leaked out through one of the old supers who had worked at the theatre for years, that room 25 had always borne the name of being haunted, and that, excepting in circumstances such as the present, it had invariably been kept locked. Some two years ago, according to the old super, when just such another emergency had occurred and the room had been used, the same thing had happened : the gentleman who had been put there had been seized with a sudden fit of madness, and had broken everything he could lay hands on ; and some time before that a similar experience had befallen an actress who had unavoidably—there being no other room available—occupied room 25.

Now had Mayhewe not heard of these two cases, he might have concluded, in spite of feeling sure that he had been in a normal state of mind upon entering the room, that what he had gone through was due merely to an over-excited imagination ;

but since he now knew that others had witnessed the same phenomena, he saw no reason to doubt that there was some peculiarly sinister influence attached to the room. As to the cause of the haunting, he could elicit nothing more authentic or definite than the somewhat vague recollections of a very old actor. According to this rather doubtful authority, shortly after the opening of the theatre, one of the performers had suddenly developed madness and had been confined in room 25 till a suitable escort had been found to take him to an asylum. It was the only tragic occurrence, he asserted, that had ever taken place in that theatre. Now, supposing this to be true—that a madman really had been conducted from the stage to room 25 and temporarily confined there —might one not reasonably believe that in this incident lay the origin of the hauntings? It was in this room, in all probability, that the outbreak of madness passed its most acute stage—that psychological stage when the rational ego makes its last desperate stand against the overwhelming assault of a new and diseased self. And again—supposing this incident to be a fact—what more likely than that the immaterial insane ego of the afflicted man would, at times, separate itself from his material body and revisit the scene of its terrible conflict, permanently taking up its abode there after its material body had passed away? This theory—a very possible one, to my mind—would have strong support from parallel cases, for half the most malignant forms of haunting are directly traceable to the earth-bound spirits of the insane. There are several houses within a short walking distance of Bond Street that were once the temporary homes of mentally afflicted people, and they are now haunted in a more or less similar manner to room 25.

If this story of the old actor's is not correct—if his memory played him false—then of course one must look around for some other solution ; and as, apparently, there is no history attached to the Prince Regent Theatre itself, one must assume either that the site of the theatre was haunted prior to the erection of the present building ; or that the ghost was originally attached to some person who once occupied room 25, and that it subsequently left that person and remained in the room ; or that some article of furniture in room 25, possibly even a fixture, was imported there from some badly haunted locality. There is, indeed, evidence regarding the first point ; evidence that, either on or close to the site of the theatre, the remains of prehistoric animals—animals of a singularly savage species, which makes it more than likely that they met with a violent death—were unearthed ; and as ghostly phenomena in the form of animals are quite as common as ghostly phenomena in the form of human beings, the hauntings of room 25 may very possibly be due to the spirit of one or more of these creatures. Or again, they might be caused by what is generally known as a Vice Elemental, or "Neutrarian" ; that is to say, a spirit that has never inhabited a material body, but which is wholly hostile to the human species. Such spirits are often, I believe, drawn to certain spots by the lustful or malicious thoughts of individuals, and this might well be the case at the Prince Regent's Theatre.

.   .   .   .

It was also during my engagement at the Mercury that I heard of a haunting at the Lombard. This theatre, it appears, has a ghostly visitant in the form of a particularly malevolent - looking clown.

According to one report, a lady and her daughter —Mrs. and Miss Dawkins—occupied box 3 one January night during the run of an exceedingly pretty modern version of *Cinderella*.

The lights were down and all eyes were focused on Cinderella, one of the prettiest and daintiest little actresses in London, dressed in pink and sitting before a very realistic make-belief of a kitchen fire, when Miss Dawkins, who had her elbows resting on the balustrade and was leaning well forward, heard a faint ejaculation from close beside her. Fearing lest her mother was ill, she turned sharply round, and was somewhat surprised to see that Mrs. Dawkins had left her seat and was leaning against the wall of the box with her arms folded and a most satirical smile on her face. Both the attitude and the expression were so entirely novel that Miss Dawkins could only conclude that her mother had suddenly taken leave of her senses ; and she was deliberating what to do, when a feeling that a sudden metamorphosis was about to take place held her spellbound. Bit by bit her mother seemed to fade away, to melt into the background ; the dim outline and the general posture remained, but instead of the actual body and well-known face, she saw something else gradually begin to form and to usurp their place. Her mother had very delicate and beautifully shaped hands, but these vanished, and the hands Miss Dawkins now looked on were large and red and coarse—horribly coarse. Fearful of what she might see next, but totally unable to fight against some strange, controlling agency, she continued to look. First, her eyes rested on a pair of sleeves—white, baggy, and soiled ; then on a broad, deep chest, also clad in white and decorated in the most fantastic manner conceivable in the centre ; then on a short, immensely thick neck ; and then on the face. The shock she now received was acute. Instinct had prepared her for something very startling, but for nothing quite so grotesque, nor so wholly at variance with the general atmosphere of the theatre. It was the painted, crinkled face of a clown—not a merry, jesting grimaldi, but a clown of a different type—a clown without a smile—a clown born and fully trained to his business in Hell. As he stood there glaring at the footlights, every feature, every atom of his person breathed out hate—hate of a nature so noxious and intense that it seemed to Miss Dawkins as if the very air were poisoned by it. Being a devout Catholic, she at once crossed herself and, although almost powerless with horror, began to pray. The face then faded till it entirely disappeared, and Miss Dawkins once again found herself gazing upon the well-known countenance of her mother.

" Why are you standing ? " she asked.

" I am sure I don't know," Mrs. Dawkins replied. " But I don't like this box. I think there is something very unpleasant about it. I haven't been myself for the last few minutes. When I was sitting by you just now, I suddenly became obsessed with a bitter hatred against everyone on the stage. The very sight of them maddened me. It seemed to me I had met them all in a former existence and that they had done me some irreparable injury. I got up and began to plot how I could best get even with them. Then the idea of setting fire to the theatre seized me. I had clear visions of a small, dimly lighted room, with which I was strangely familiar, down below the stage in a dark, draughty basement. I knew every inch of the place as if I had lived there all my life. ' I will go there,' I said to myself, ' and apply a match. If anyone sees me, no one will suspect. They will only say, " It's old Tom. He didn't get the chuck after all. He's come back." ' I was repeating the words ' It's old Tom,' and ' Fire,' when something seemed to strike me very forcibly on the forehead. This caused me the greatest agony for a moment. Then you spoke, and I was myself again."

" Would you like to go home ? " Miss Dawkins asked anxiously.

" I think I would," was the response. And they went.

Subsequently, a few judicious inquiries elicited no little light on the matter.

Many years before, an old actor, called Tom Weston, had been employed annually in pantomime at the Lombard as clown. Like so many of his profession, however, particularly the older ones, he took to drink ; and he was so often intoxicated on the stage that the management were at last obliged to dismiss him. He took his dismissal very badly, and one night, having gone to the theatre in disguise, he was discovered in the act of setting fire to a room immediately beneath the stage. In consideration for his many years' service and age, the management did not prosecute, but recommended his friends to keep him under close supervision. Tom, however, very soon ceased to cause the management any anxiety, for, two days after he had attempted, in so diabolical a manner, to wreak his vengeance on all who had been associated with him at the theatre, he shot himself dead in his own home. But on every anniversary of his death, so it is affirmed, he is either seen or heard, or his presence is in some way demonstrated, in box 3 of the Lombard Theatre. That his spirit should frequent that particular spot in the theatre seems to be a fact for which no reason can be assigned.

CHAPTER VI

THE RETICULE

BETWEEN Norwich and Swaffham, low down in a little valley, there once stood a mill. It is now a ruin, and all the people round studiously avoid it after nightfall. It must be admitted that they have some reason for doing so in view of the incidents I am about to relate.

Some years ago on an early autumn afternoon two ladies, Miss Smith and Miss Raven, fashion designers to the firm of Kirsome & Gooting, Sloane Street, London, set out from Norwich for a tramp into the country. Both girls—for they were only girls—were typically modern ; that is to say, they were bonny and athletic, and, despite the sedentary nature of their vocation, extremely fond of outdoor life. Miss Raven, the elder of the two, was nice-looking without perhaps being actually pretty ; but Miss Smith was undeniably a beauty. Had she been a lady of title or an actress, all the society papers would have been full of her. She did not, however, crave for notoriety ; she was quite content with the homage of most of the young men whom she knew, and the unspoken admiration of many men whom she did not know, but who looked at her out of doors or sat near to her in theatres and restaurants.

She was much attached to Miss Raven, and as the two strode along, swinging their arms, their tongues wagged merrily and without intermission. On and on, down one hill and up another, past wood and brook and hamlet they went, till a gradual fading of the light warned them it was about time to think of turning back.

" We must go as far as that old ruin," Miss Raven said, pointing to a tumble-down white building that nestled close to a winding stream. " I've never seen anything quite so picturesque."

" And I've never seen anything quite so weird," Miss Smith replied. " I'm not at all sure I like it. Besides, I'm desperately thirsty. I want my tea. We'd much better go home."

They had an argument, and it was eventually agreed that they should go on—but not beyond a certain point. " Not an inch farther, mind," Miss Smith said, " or I'll turn back and leave you."

The ruin lay in a hollow, and as the two girls descended the slope leading to it, a mist rose from the ground as if to greet them. They quickened their steps, and, approaching nearer, perceived a mill wheel—the barest skeleton, crowned with moss and ferns and dripping with slime. The pool into which it dripped was overgrown in places with reeds and chickweed, but was singularly bare and black in the centre, and suggestive of very great depth. Weeping willows bordered the stream, and their sloping, stunted forms were gradually growing more and more indistinct in the oncoming mist.

The space in front of the house, once, no doubt, a prettily cultivated garden, was now full of rank grass and weeds, and dotted here and there with unsightly mounds consisting of fallen bricks and mortar. Some of these mounds, long, low, and narrow, were unpleasantly suggestive of graves, whilst the atmosphere of the place, the leaden-hued and mystic atmosphere, charged to the utmost with the smell of decayed trees and mouldy walls, might well have been that of an ancient church-yard.

A sense of insufferable gloom, utterly different from any they had ever before experienced, took possession of the two girls.

" This place depresses me horribly. I don't know when I've felt so sad," Miss Smith observed. " It's very stupid of me, I know, but I can't help thinking some great tragedy must have taken place here."

" I feel rather like that too," Miss Raven responded. " I've never seen such dreariness. Do you see those shadows on the water ? How strange they are ! There's nothing that I can see to account for them. There's certainly nothing the least like them in the sedge. Besides, there oughtn't to be any shadows there. There are none anywhere else. Look ! Oh, do look ! They are changing. They are completely different now. See, I'll throw a stone at them." Her throw, missing its mark, was so characteristically girlish that Miss Smith, despite her leanings to suffragism, laughed. Miss

Raven threw again, and this time a deep plomb announced her success. " There," she cried triumphantly. " Now do you see it ? "

" I see something," Miss Smith answered. Then, with sudden eagerness : " Yes, you are right. The shadows are continually changing. They seem to separate themselves from the sedge, and fall like live things into the pool. By the way, the pool seems to be growing darker and bigger. I don't like the place at all. For Heaven's sake let's get away from it ! "

Miss Raven, however, was too fascinated. Stepping carefully, so as to avoid the mud and long grass, she went right up to the pool and peered into it.

" How fearfully deep and still it is," she said. " What a beastly place to end one's days in." Then she gave a sudden cry. " Aileen ! Here ! Come here, quick ! "

Miss Smith hastened up to her. " What is it ? " she said. " How you frightened me ! "

Miss Raven pointed excitedly at the water. It was no longer tranquil. The chickweed round the edges began to oscillate, white bubbles formed in the centre, and then, quite suddenly, the entire surface became a seething, hissing, rushing, roaring whirlpool, which commenced rising in the most hideous and menacing manner. Seizing Miss Raven by the arm, Miss Smith dragged her back, and the two fled in terror. The fog, however, was so thick that they missed their way. They failed to strike the road, and, instead, found themselves plunging deeper and deeper into a fearful quagmire of mud and the rankest compound of rushes, weeds, and grass.

They were just despairing of ever extricating themselves when Miss Smith felt a light tap on her shoulder, and swinging round, was almost startled out of her senses at the sight of a very white face glaring at her. Miss Raven, noticing that her companion had stopped, also turned round ; and she too received a shock. The face she saw was so very white ; the eyes—intently fixed on Miss Smith—so strangely luminous ; the head—covered with red, shaggy hair—so disproportionately large ; and the figure—that of a hunchback youth—as a whole so extraordinarily grotesque.

He made no sound, but, signing to them to follow him, he began to move away with a queer, shambling gait. The girls, thankful enough to have found a guide, however strange, kept close at his heels, and soon found themselves once again on the roadway. Here their conductor came to a halt, and producing from under his coat what looked like a lady's reticule, he was about to thrust it into Miss Smith's hand when their eyes met, and, to her intense astonishment, he uttered a bitter cry of disappointment and vanished. His action and disappearance were so inexplicable that the girls, completely demoralised, took to their heels and ran without stopping till the ruins were far in their rear, and they were well on their way home.

They related their experience to the people with whom they were staying, and were then told for the first time that the ruin was well known to be

6

haunted. "Nothing will persuade any of the villagers to visit the mill pond after dusk," their hostess remarked, "especially at this time of the year, when they declare the water suddenly rises and follows them. The place has a most sinister reputation, and certainly several people, to my knowledge, have committed suicide there. The last to do so was Davy Dyer, the hunchback, whose ghost you must have just seen. His was rather a sad case, as I have good reason to know. Would you like to hear it ? "

The girls eagerly assented, and their hostess told them as follows :

" Ten years ago there stood on the spot you visited this afternoon a very picturesque house called the ' Gyp Mill.' It was then extremely old, and as its foundations were faulty, it was thought a severe storm would, sooner or later, completely demolish it. Partly for this reason, and partly because the mill pool was said to be haunted, it stood for a long time untenanted. At last it was taken by a widow named Dyer. Mrs. Dyer was quite a superior kind of person. She had at one time, I believe, kept a fairly good class girls' school in Bury St. Edmunds, but losing her connection through illness, she had been obliged to think of some other means of gaining a livelihood. When she came to the Gyp Mill she cultivated the garden and sold its produce ; provided teas for picnic parties in the summer ; and let out rooms, chiefly to artists.

" She had one son, Davy, a very intelligent boy of about eighteen, but hopelessly deformed. He

was not only hunchbacked but he had an abnormally large head ; and what was quite unpardon-
able in the eyes of the village children, who
tormented him shamefully, a mass of the brightest
red hair.

" Well, one day, a girl whom I will call Beryl
Denver, came to stay with me. Beryl was extremely
pretty and horribly spoilt. She had gone on the
stage against her parents' wishes and had been
an immediate success. At the time I am speaking
of she had just had an offer of marriage from a
duke, and it was to hear what I had to say about
it—for I am, I think, the only person from whom
she ever asks advice—that she was paying me this
visit. After being with me three days, however,
and changing her mind with regard to the duke's
offer at least a dozen times, she suddenly announced that she must seek some more countrified
place to stay in. ' I want to go right away from
everywhere,' she said, ' so that I can forget—
forget that there is such a place as London. Don't
you know of any pretty cottage or picturesque
old farm, near here, that I could stay at ? '

" I suggested the Gyp Mill, and she started off
at once to look at it.

" She came back full of enthusiasm. ' It's a
delightful spot,' she said. ' I'm glad I went to
see it—the flowers are lovely, and the old woman's
a dear—but I couldn't stay there. I couldn't
stand that hunchback son of hers. His white face
and big dark eyes alarmed me horribly. I don't
think it's at all right he should be at large.'

" ' Poor Davy,' I remarked. ' His appearance is certainly against him, but I can assure you he is absolutely harmless. I know him well.'

" Beryl shook her head. ' You know my views, Aunty,' she said (she always calls me Aunty although I am not related to her in any way). ' All ugly people have a kink of badness in them somewhere. They must be either cruel, or spiteful, or treacherous, or, in some way or other, evilly disposed. I am quite certain that looks reflect the mind. No, I couldn't endure that boy. I can't stay there.'

" In the morning, however, as I had fully anticipated, she changed her mind. A fly was sent for, and she drove off to the Gyp Mill, taking all her luggage with her. How Mrs. Dyer ever got it up her narrow staircase I can't think, but she must have managed it somehow, for Beryl stayed and, contrary to my expectations, for more than one night.

" Davy, she afterwards informed me, soon got on her nerves. Always when she went out she caught him covertly peeping at her from behind the window curtain of the little front parlour ; and if ever she stood for a moment to chat with his mother, she could see him slyly watching her through a chink in the doorway. She had seldom, so far, met him out of doors ; but as she was returning from a walk one afternoon, she came across a group of village children shouting at and jostling someone very roughly in their midst, and approaching nearer saw that the object of their

abuse was Davy, and that, in addition to pushing
and pummelling him, they were tormenting him
with stinging nettles—a very favourite device of
the children in this district. Filled with disgust,
rather than pity (Beryl, like most modern girls,
is wanting in real sentiment, and in this instance
simply hated to think that anyone could derive
amusement from so ungainly a creature), she
interfered.

" ' You abominable little wretches ! ' she cried.
' Leave him alone at once. Do you hear ? '

" Had a bomb fallen, the children could not have
been more surprised. One or two of the boys
were inclined to be rude, but on the rest the effect
of Beryl's looks and clothes (the latter in particular)
was magical. Gazing at her open-mouthed, they
drew back and allowed Davy to continue his way.

" After this, Davy peeped more than ever, and
Beryl, losing patience, determined to put a stop
to it. Catching him in the act of following her
through the fields one morning, she turned on him
in a fury.

" ' How dare you ? ' she demanded. ' How dare
you annoy me like this ? Go home at once.'

" ' This is my home, lady,' Davy replied, his
eyes on the ground and his cheeks crimson.

" ' Then you must choose some other route,'
Beryl retorted ; ' and for goodness' sake don't be
everlastingly looking at me. I can't stand it. No
wonder those children rounded on you, you——'
She was going to call him some very strong name—
for Beryl when roused didn't stick at trifles—but

suddenly checked herself. She began to realise that this queer, distorted little object was in love with her. Now no girl in London, probably, had more admirers than Beryl. Peers, politicians, authors, men of all vocations and classes had succumbed to her beauty, and she had deemed herself pretty well blasé. But here was a novelty. A poor, ostracised rustic hunchback—the incarnation of ugliness and simplicity. 'You know how the horrible often fascinates one,' she said to me later, 'for instance, a nasty tooth, or some other equally horrible defect in a person's face, which one keeps on looking at however much one tries not to—well, it was a fascination of this kind that possessed me now. I felt I must see more of the hunchback and egg him on to the utmost.'

" Apparently it was owing to this fascination that Beryl, changing her tactics, encouraged Davy to talk to her, and assuming an interest in the garden, which she knew was his one hobby, gradually drew him out. Very shy and embarrassed at first, he could only very briefly answer her questions ; but soon deceived by her manner—for Beryl could act just as cleverly off the stage as on it—he grew bolder, and talked well on his favourite subject, natural history. He really knew a great deal, and Beryl, despite the fact that she could hardly tell the difference between a hollyhock and marigold, couldn't help being impressed.

" She walked home with him that day ; and for days afterwards she was often to be seen in his company.

" ' He'll miss you dreadfully when you go, ma'am,' Mrs. Dyer said to her. ' He thinks the world of you. He told me last night that he only wished he could do something to show you how grateful he is for your kindness to him.' Of course, Mrs. Dyer did not say that Davy was in love—but Beryl knew it. She knew that to him she was a deified being and that he absolutely adored her. Thus matters stood, when a letter from the duke made Beryl decide to leave Gyp Mill at once and return with all speed to London. She walked to the post office to dispatch a telegram, and Davy went with her. Beryl knew that this would be the last time, in all probability, that she would ever walk with him ; and feeling that she must find out how far his love for her had progressed she agreed to his proposal that they should return home by a rather longer route. He wished, he said, to show her a garden which was by far the prettiest in all the country round, and it would not take them more than a quarter of a mile or so out of their way. Of course Beryl looked upon this suggestion as a mere pretext on Davy's part for prolonging the walk, and she wondered whether he would say anything, or whether his passion would be held in check by his natural respect for her superior social position. She was disappointed. Although she saw love for her shining more brightly than ever in his eyes, he did not speak of it ; he talked only of flowers and of the great beauties of nature. Bored to distraction, she at last cut him short, and, declaring that she had no time to waste, hurried on. It was not until they had reached home that she discovered she had lost her reticule, containing not only a purse full of sovereigns but the letter she had just received from the duke. She distinctly remembered having it with her, she said, when Davy was prosing over the stupid flowers, and she supposed she must have left it somewhere in the garden, probably on the seat where they had sat for a few minutes. Davy, of course, went back at once to look for it, but when he returned an hour or so later and in crestfallen tones told her that he could not find it, her anger knew no bounds. She did not actually call him a fool, but she made him clearly understand she thought him one ; and he set off again almost immediately to have another look for it. He did not come back this time till close on midnight, and he had not the courage to tell her of his failure. His mother did it for him. Beryl went away early the following morning, too indignant to shake hands with either Mrs. Dyer or her son. ' If Davy didn't actually take the reticule,' she wrote to me some days later, ' it was all owing to him—to his bothering me to see that rotten garden—that I lost it ; but I firmly believe he has it. Ugly faces, you know, are indicative of ugly minds—of a bad kink somewhere.'

" Of course the affair of the reticule soon became public property. It was advertised for in the local papers, and the woman in the post office told everybody that she remembered seeing it in Beryl's hand when she left the shop. ' Davy,' she said, ' was with Miss Denver at the time, and I particularly noticed that he walked very close to her and watched her in a peculiarly furtive manner.'

" Now the villagers, with whom the Dyers had always been unpopular, were not slow in taking up the cue, and consequently Davy, now waylaid by armies of children calling him thief, and even beating him, never had a moment's peace.

" At last he was found one morning in the mill-pond drowned, and it was generally believed that remorse for his sins had made him commit suicide. His mother alone thought otherwise. I did not see Beryl nor hear anything of her for at least two years after Davy's death, when to my surprise she drove up to the door one day with her usual pile of luggage.

" ' Who is it this time ? ' I said, after we had exchanged greetings. ' The duke again ! '

" ' Oh dear no,' Beryl replied. ' I broke it off definitely with him long ago. He was too boring for words, always dangling after me and never letting me go out with anyone else. If he had been tolerably good-looking I might have stood it, but he wasn't. He was hopelessly plain. However, I made some use of him, and he certainly gave me good presents. I have been engaged several times since, and I've come now to ask your advice about the Earl of C——'s eldest son. Shall I marry him or not ? Do you think he's worth it ? '

" I did not answer her at once, but let her ramble on, till she suddenly turned to me and said, ' Do you remember the last time I was here ? Two years ago ! You know I stayed at that delightful old mill house—the Gyp something, and lost my reticule. Well, I found it some time afterwards in my hat-box. I hadn't taken it out with me that day after all. And I could have sworn I had. Wasn't it funny ? '

" ' Extraordinary, perhaps,' I remarked, with rather more severity in my voice than I had ever used to her before, ' but hardly funny.' And I was about to relate to her all that had occurred in the interim, when something checked me. After all, I thought, it would be just as well for this spoilt, heartless little London actress to go to the Gyp Mill and find out for herself.

" ' Oh, I suppose I ought to have written to the people and let them know,' she said carelessly, ' but I was really too busy. I always have such lots to do. Such heaps of correspondence to attend to, and so many visits to make. If it's a fine day to-morrow I'll walk over and explain.'

" I did not, of course, expect Beryl would go, but greatly to my surprise, soon after luncheon, she came into my bedroom in her hat and coat. ' I'm off,' she said. ' I think the walk will do me good. And, look here, don't wait dinner for me, because in all probability I'll stay the night. It all depends upon how I feel. If I'm not back by eight you need not expect me till to-morrow. Bye-bye.'

" She stole to my side and kissed me, and, armed with an umbrella and mackintosh, set off up the street. I watched her till she turned the corner. Then I lay down and wondered what sort of a reception she would meet with at the hands of Mrs.

Dyer. As the afternoon waned the sky grew ominously dark, and the wind rose. Presently big drops of rain spluttered against the window, and there was every indication of a very severe storm. Had Beryl been on good terms with Mrs. Dyer my mind would have been at rest, as she would have been able to take refuge at the Mill, but, knowing Mrs. Dyer's feelings towards her, I doubted very much if Mrs. Dyer would allow her to set foot within the house ; and she would have some distance to walk before she could reach another shelter.

"Down came the rain in grim earnest, and that night witnessed the worst storm Norwich had known for many years. Beryl did not return. I sat up till twelve wondering what had become of her— for despite this wayward child's many faults I was much attached to her—and slept very little for the rest of the night. In the morning my maid came into my room in a breathless state of excitement.

" 'Oh, mum,' she exclaimed, 'the storm has destroyed half Norfolk.' (This, of course, I knew to be an exaggeration.) 'What do you think! Simkins' Store is blowed down, nearly all the chimneypots are off in Fore Street, and the milkman has just told me the Gyp Mill is under water and Mrs. Dyer is drowned!'

" 'What!' I shrieked. 'The Gyp Mill under water! Are you sure? Miss Denver was staying there last night. Call a cab—I must go there at once.'

"The maid flew ; and I was feverishly scrambling into my clothes, when, to my utmost relief, in walked Beryl.

" ' So you've heard,' she said, looking rather pale, but otherwise quite composed. ' The Gyp Mill valley is under water, and old Mrs. Dyer is drowned. It was rather lucky for me that I didn't go there after all, wasn't it ? Quite a narrow escape, in fact.'

" ' Thank God, you're safe ! ' I exclaimed, drawing her into my arms and kissing her frantically. ' Tell me all about it.'

" ' Oh, there isn't much to tell,' she said. ' When I got a mile or two on the road I found I had quite forgotten the way, so I inquired of the first person I met, a labourer, and he said, " When you come to the duck pond bear sharply to your left." Well, I trudged on and on, and I am sure I must have gone miles, but no duck pond ; and I was beginning to despair of ever seeing it, when a sudden swerve in the road revealed it to me. The sky was very dark and threatening, and the wind—you know how I detest wind—sorely tried my temper. It was perfectly fiendish. Well, when I got to the pond I found there were two roads and I had quite forgotten which of them I had to take. I was standing there shivering, feeling horribly bored, when to my joy a figure suddenly hove in view. It had grown so dark that I could not make out whether the stranger was a man or a woman. Besides, I couldn't see a face at all, only a short, squat body clad in some sort of ill-fitting fustian garment. I shouted out, " Can you tell me the way to the Gyp Mill ? " but could get no reply. The strange creature simply put out one hand, and taking the road to the right, beckoned to me to follow. Then I suddenly remembered that the other person—the labouring man—had told me to take the road to the left, and I ran after the curious-looking individual shouting, "The Gyp Mill.—Do you hear?—I want to go to the Gyp Mill. Mrs. Dyer's." Again I got no response, but the hand waved me on more vigorously than before.

" ' It was now so dark that I could hardly see where I was treading, and the wind was so strong that I had the greatest difficulty in keeping my feet. I battled on, however, and after what seemed to me an eternity, we eventually stopped outside a building that showed a twinkling light in one of the windows. My conductor opened a wicket gate and, signing to me to follow, walked me up a narrow winding path to the front door. Here he halted and, turning suddenly round on me, showed his face. It was the Dyer boy—Davy, I think they called him. Davy the hunchback.' Here Beryl paused.

" ' Are you quite sure ? ' I asked.

" ' Absolutely,' she replied. ' I couldn't mistake him. There he was—with his hunchback, huge head, cheeks looking whiter than ever—and red hair. How I could see that it was red in the dark I can't tell you, but all the same I could, and moreover, the colour was very clear and distinct. Well, he stood and looked at me for some seconds beseechingly, and then said something—but so quickly I couldn't catch what it was. I told him so, and he repeated it, jabber, jabber, jabber. Then

I grew angry. "Why have you brought me here?"
I shouted. "I wanted to go to the Gyp Mill."
He spoke again in the same incomprehensible way,
and holding out his hands as if to implore my forgiveness, suddenly disappeared. Where he went
to is a mystery. The rain had now begun to fall in
torrents, and to attempt to go on was madness.
Consequently, I rapped at the door and asked the
woman who opened it if she could put me up for the
night. "Yes, miss," she said. "We have a spare
room, if you don't mind it's being rather small.
The gentleman that has been staying here left this
morning. Did anyone recommend you?" "Mr.
Dyer brought me here," I said, "and, I believe, he
is somewhere outside." "Mr. Dyer!" the woman
exclaimed, looking at me in the oddest manner.
"I don't know a Mr. Dyer. Who do you mean?"
"Why, Davy Dyer," I replied, "the son of the old
woman who lives at the Mill. Davy Dyer, the
hunchback."

"'Then, to my amazement, the woman caught
me by the arm. "Davy Dyer, the hunchback!"
she cried. "Why, miss, you must either be
dreaming or mad. Davy Dyer drowned himself in
the Mill pool two years ago!"'"

CHAPTER VII

THE COOMBE

A CASE OF A WILTSHIRE ELEMENTAL

PEOPLE are not half particular enough about new houses. So long as the soil is gravel, so long as the rooms are large and airy, the wall-papers artistic, and there's no basement, the rest does not matter ; at least not as a rule. Few think of ghosts or of superphysical influences. And yet the result of such a consideration is what would probably weigh most with me in selecting a newly built house. But then, I have had disagreeable experiences, and others I know have had them too.

Let me quote, for example, what befell my old acquaintance, Fitzsimmons. Robert Fitzsimmons was for years editor of the *Daily Gossip*, but finally retired from the post owing to ill health. His doctor recommended him some quiet, restful place in the country, so he decided to migrate to Wiltshire. After scouring the county for some time, he alighted on a spot, not very far from Devizes, that attracted him immensely.

It was prettily wooded, at least he called it prettily wooded, within easy walking distance of

the village of Arkabye, and about a quarter of a
mile from the site of an ancient barrow that had
just been removed to make way for several cottages.
Fitzsimmons loved beeches, particularly copper
beeches, which he noticed flourished here exceedingly, and the thought of living surrounded by
these trees gave him infinite satisfaction. He
finally bought a small piece of land in the coombe,
getting it freehold at a ridiculously low figure, and
erected a house on it, which he called " Shane
Garth " after a remote ancestor.

The first month seems to have passed quite uneventfully. It was true the children, Bobbie and
Jane, said they heard noises, and declared someone always came and tapped against their window
after they were in bed ; but Fitzsimmons attributed
these disturbances to mice and bats with which
the coombe was infested. One thing, however,
greatly disturbed his wife and himself, and that
was the naughtiness of the children. Prior to
their coming to the new house they had been as
good as gold and had got on extremely well together ; but the change of surroundings seemed
to have wrought in them a complete change of
character.

They were continually getting into mischief of
some sort, and hardly a day passed that they did
not quarrel and fight, and always in a remarkably
vindictive manner. Bobbie would creep up behind Jane, and pull her hair and pinch her, whilst
Jane in revenge would break Bobbie's toys and do
something nasty to him while he slept.

Then their language was so bad. They used expressions that shocked everyone in the house, and no one could say where they had picked them up. But worst of all was their cruelty to animals. The nurse came to Mrs. Fitzsimmons one morning to show her a fowl that was limping across the yard in great pain. Bobbie had pelted it with stones and broken its leg.

He was punished ; but the very next day he and Jane were caught inflicting the most abominable tortures on a mouse. Jane rivalled the Chinese in the ingenuity of her cruelties. She scalded insects very slowly to death, and scandalised the village children by showing them a rabbit and sundry smaller animals which she had vivisected and skinned alive.

One does occasionally hear of epidemics of cruelty breaking out in certain districts. A year or two ago, cats came in for especially bad treatment in the neighbourhood of Red Lion Square, and the culprits, girls as well as boys, were invariably excused, it being suggested that the war had excited their naturally high spirits. I remember, too, in Cornwall, not so very long ago, children being seized with a mania for torturing birds. They caught them with fish-hooks, and never grew tired of watching them choke and writhe and otherwise distort themselves in their death agonies. In Wales, too, there are periodical outbursts of similar passions. Some years ago a child was prosecuted in South Wales for pulling a live rabbit in half ; but the magistrates acquitted the accused on the

7

plea that it was only following the example of nearly
all the other children in the district. ˙ Well, Robert
Fitzsimmons wondered if his children had fallen
victims to one of these epidemics, and he suggested
to his wife that they should be sent away to a
boarding school. To his astonishment, however,
Mrs. Fitzsimmons took a more lenient view of their
conduct.

" It's no use being too hard on them," she said.
" I don't believe for one moment that Bobbie and
Jane realise that animals can feel as we do—that
human beings have not the monopoly of the nervous
system. We must get a governess—someone who
can explain things to them with tact and patience,
and not get out of temper, like you do, Robert.
The children must be treated with kindness and
sympathy."

Fitzsimmons could hardly believe that it was his
wife speaking ; she had been such a keen champion
of animals, and had boxed the ears of more than one
London ragamuffin whom she had caught ill-treating
a dog or cat. However, he gave way, and agreed
that the children should be committed to the care
of a benevolent old lady whom Mrs. Fitzsimmons
knew, and who might be engaged as governess and
domiciled in the house. This matter was barely
settled when Mr. Merryweather, an artist friend of
Robert Fitzsimmons, came to stay at Shane Garth,
and it was on the evening after his arrival that
Fitzsimmons first came to realise that the coombe
was haunted. He had been out all day fishing,
alone, his friend, Merryweather, being engaged

painting a portrait of Mrs. Fitzsimmons and Jane; and the evening having well set in, he was now on his way home. Passing the site of the ancient barrow, he could see in the hollow beneath him the welcome lights of Shane Garth. He paused for a moment to refill his pipe, and then commenced to descend into the coombe. It was an exquisite night, the air warm and fragrant with the scent of newly mown hay, the moon full, and the sky one mass of scintillating stars. Fitzsimmons was enchanted. Again and again he threw back his head and drew in the air in great gulps. When halfway down the hill, however, he became aware of a sudden change; the atmosphere was no longer light and exhilarating, but dark, heavy, and oppressive.

He noticed, too, that there were strange lights and that the shadows that flickered to and fro the broad highway continually came and went, and differed, in some strangely subtle fashion, from any shadows he had ever seen before. But what attracted his attention even more was a tree—a tall tree with a trunk of the most peculiar colour. In the quick-changing light of the coombe it looked yellow—a lurid yellow streaked with black after the nature of a tiger's skin—and Fitzsimmons never remembered seeing it there before. He halted for a moment to look at it more intently, and it seemed to him to change its position. He rubbed his eyes to make sure he was not dreaming and looked again. Yes, without a doubt it was nearer to the roadway, and very gradually it was getting nearer still.

Moreover, although the night was still, so still that hardly a leaf of any of the other trees quivered, its branches were in a state of the most violent agitation.

Fitzsimmons was not normally nervous, and on the subject of the superphysical he was decidedly sceptical ; but he could not help admitting that it was queer, and he began to wonder whether there was not some other way of getting home. Ashamed, however, of his cowardice, he at length made up his mind to look closer at the tree, and ascertain if possible the cause of its remarkable behaviour. He advanced towards it, and it moved again. This time the moonlight threw it into such strong relief that it stood out with photographic clearness, every detail in its composition most vividly portrayed.

What exactly he saw, Fitzsimmons has never been prevailed upon to say. All one can get out of him is " that it had the semblance to a tree, but that the semblance was quite superficial. It was in reality something quite different, and that the difference was so marked and unexpected that he was immeasurably shocked." I asked Fitzsimmons why he was shocked, and he said, " By the obscenity of the thing—by its unparalleled beastliness." He would not say any more. It took him several minutes to sum up courage to pass it, and all the while it stood close to the roadside waiting for him. Fitzsimmons had been a tolerably good athlete in his youth—he won the open hundred at school—and though well over forty, he was spare and tough, and as sound as a bell with regard to his heart and lungs. Bracing himself up, he made a sudden dash, and had passed it, by some dozen or so yards, when he heard something drop with a soft plumb, and the next minute there came the quick patter of bare feet in hot pursuit. Frightened as he was, Fitzsimmons does not think his terror was quite so great as his feeling of utter loathing and abhorrence. He felt if the thing touched him, however slightly, he would be contaminated body and soul, and would never be able to look a decent person in the face again.

Hence his sprint was terrific—faster, he thinks, than he ever did in the school Close—and he kept praying too all the while.

But the thing gained on him, and he feels certain it would have been all up with him, had not a party of cyclists suddenly appeared on the scene and scared it off. He heard it go back pattering up the coombe, and there was something about those sounds that told him more plainly than words that he had not seen the last of it, and that it would come to him again. When he entered the house he encountered Merryweather and his wife together, and he could not help noticing that they seemed on strangely familiar terms and very upset and startled at seeing him. He spoke to his wife about it afterwards, and though she vehemently denied there was any truth in his suspicions, she could not meet his gaze with her customary frankness. Merryweather was the last person on earth he would have suspected of flirting with anyone,

and up to the present time Mrs. Robert Fitzsimmons
had always behaved with the utmost propriety
and decorum ; indeed, everyone regarded her as
a model wife and mother, and particular, even to
prudishness.

The incident worried Fitzsimmons a great deal,
and for nights he lay awake thinking about
it.

The governess was the next person to experience
the hauntings. Her room was a sort of attic,
large and full of quaint angles, and it looked out on
to the coombe. Well, one night she had gone to
bed rather early, owing to a very bad headache
which had been brought on by the behaviour of
the children, who had been naughty with a naughtiness that could scarcely have been surpassed in
hell, and was partly undressed when her eyes
suddenly became centred on the wall-paper, which
had a curious dark pattern running through
it.

She looked at the pattern, and it suddenly took
the form of a tree. Now some people are in the
habit of seeing faces where others see nothing.
The governess belonged to the latter category.
She was absolutely practical and matter-of-fact,
a typical Midland farmer's daughter, and had no
imagination whatever. Consequently, when she
saw the tree, she at once regarded it in the light
of some peculiar phenomenon, and stared at it in
open-mouthed astonishment. At first it was simply
a tree, a tree with a well-defined trunk and branches.
Soon, however, the trunk became a vivid yellow

and black, a most unpleasant, virulent yellow, and the branches seemed to move. Much alarmed, she shrank away from it and clutched hold of the bed. She afterwards declared that the tree suddenly became something quite different, something she never dare even think of, and which nothing in God's world would ever make her mention. She made one supreme effort to reach the bell, just touched it with the tips of her fingers, and then sank on the bed in a dead swoon.

She told her story next morning to Mrs. Fitzsimmons, and although asked on no account to breathe a word of it to the children, she told them too. That night she took her departure, and Mrs. Fitzsimmons refused her a character.

Curious noises were now frequently heard in the house. Door handles turned and footsteps tiptoed cautiously about the hall and passages at about two o'clock in the morning.

Mrs. Fitzsimmons was the next to have a nasty experience. Going to her room one evening, when everyone else was at supper, she saw the bed valance suddenly move. Thinking it was the cat, she bent down, and was about to call " Puss," when a huge striped thing, shaped, so she thought, something like the trunk of a much gnarled tree, shot out and, rolling swiftly past her, vanished in the wainscoting. She called out, and Fitzsimmons, who came running up, found her leaning against the doorway of their room, laughing hysterically.

Two days later, on his return from another fishing expedition, he found that his wife had gone, leaving a note for him pinned to the dressing-table.

"You won't see me again," she wrote. "I'm off with Dicky Merryweather. We have discovered we love one another, and that life apart would be simply unendurable. Take care of the children, and try and make them forget me. Get them away from here, if you possibly can. I attribute every-thing — my changed feelings towards you, and Bobbie and Jane's naughtiness—to the presence of that beastly thing."

. . . .

Of course it was a terrible blow to Fitzsimmons, and he told me that if it had not been for the children he would have committed suicide there and then. He was devotedly attached to his wife, and the thought that she no longer cared for him made him yearn to die.

However, Bobbie and Jane were dependent on him, and for their sakes he determined to go on living.

A week passed—to Fitzsimmons the saddest and dreariest of his life—and he once again came tramping home in the twilight.

Not troubling now whether he saw the ghost or not, for there was no one to care whether he was good or bad, or what became of him, he slouched through the coombe with his long stride more marked and apparent than usual. On nearing the house and noticing that there was no bright light, such as he had been accustomed to, in any of the front windows, but only the feeble flare of the oil lamp over the front door, a terrible feeling of loneliness came over him. He let himself in. The hall was in semi-darkness, and he could hear no sounds from the kitchen. He could see a glimmer of light, however, issuing from under the kitchen door, and he promptly steered for it. The cook, Agatha, was sitting in front of the fire, reading a sixpenny novel.

" Why is the house in darkness ? " Fitzsimmons asked angrily. " Surely it is dinner-time."

The cook yawned, and looking up at Fitzsimmons, said : " It's not my place to light up. It's Rosalie's."

" Where is Rosalie ? " Fitzsimmons demanded.

" I don't know," the cook replied. " I can't be expected to know everything. The cooking's enough for me—at least for the wages I get. Rosalie's been gone somewhere for the last two hours. I haven't seen or heard anything of her since tea."

" And the children ? " Fitzsimmons inquired.

" Oh, the children's all right," the cook answered— " at least I suppose so ; and, you bet, they'd have let me know fast enough if they hadn't been. I don't know which of the two hollers loudest."

" Well, get my supper, for mercy's sake, for I'm famishing," Fitzsimmons said ; and he stalked back again into the darkness.

After groping about the hall for some time and knocking over a good few things, he at length put his hands on a match-box, and lighting a candle made straight for the nursery. The children had got into bed partially undressed, and were sound asleep, with their heads well buried under the bedclothes. Fitzsimmons contrived to uncover their, faces without waking them, and kissing them both lightly on the forehead, he left them and went downstairs to his study. Here he drew up a chair close to the fire and, throwing himself into it, prepared to wait till the gong sounded for supper. A slight noise in the room made him look round. Across the window recess, from which the sound apparently came, a pair of heavy red curtains were tightly drawn. Fitzsimmons rather wondered at this, because Rosalie did not usually draw the curtains before she lighted up ; so he was still looking at them and wondering, when they were suddenly shaken so violently that the metal rings made a loud rattling and jarring on the brass pole to which they were attached. Fitzsimmons watched in breathless anticipation. Every second he expected to see the curtains part and some ghoulish face peering out at him. Drawn curtains so often suggest lurking horrors of that description. Instead, however, the curtains only grew more and more agitated, shaking violently as if they had the ague. Then, all of a sudden, they were still. Fitzsimmons rose and was about to look behind them, when they started trembling again, and the one nearest the fireplace began to bulge out in the middle. Fitzsimmons stared at it with a sickening sense of foreboding. At first it had no definite form, but, very gradually, it assumed a shape, the shape he felt it would, and moved nearer him. For some seconds he was too overcome with horror to do anything, but his recollections of what it had looked like in the coombe that night, and his utter detestation of it, increased his fear, and in a frenzy of rage he snatched up a revolver from the mantelpiece and fired at it. Fitzsimmons thinks it was the bullet that made it suddenly collapse ; but I am inclined to think it was the sound of the report—as sound undoubtedly does, at times, bring about dematerialisation. There are, I think, certain sounds that generate vibrations in the air favourable to the manifestation of spirits, and other sounds that create vibratory motion destructive to the composition of what are termed ghosts. And here was an instance of the latter. Fitzsimmons waited for a few minutes, until he felt sure the thing was gone altogether, entirely quit of the premises, and then, revolver in hand, pulled aside the curtains.

The next moment he reeled back, stupefied with horror. Lying at full length on the floor, her white face turned towards him, with a hideous grin of agony on her lips, was Rosalie.

" Good God ! " Fitzsimmons said to himself. " Good God ! I've killed her. What in Heaven's name can I do ? "

He deliberated shooting himself ; and then the cries of the children, who had been wakened by the noise, reminding him of his duties to them, he grew calmer, and telephoned at once for the nearest doctor. The latter, happening to be at home, was speedily on the spot.

"You say you shot her," he remarked to Fitz-simmons, after he had examined the body very carefully. "You must be dreaming, sir. There's not the slightest sign of any bullet. Moreover, the girl's been dead at least two hours. From the look of her, I should say she died from strychnine poisoning."

The doctor was right. The girl's death was due to strychnine, and from the bottle that was found in her possession and a message she scribbled on the study wall, there is no doubt whatever she committed suicide. "I was a nice enough girl till I came here," she wrote, "but it's the coombe that's done it. Mother warned me against it. Coombes make everyone bad."

After this, Fitzsimmons decided to clear out. Indeed, he could hardly have done otherwise, for Shane Garth was now placed under a rigorous ban. Agatha left—she did not even wait till the morning, but cleared out the same night—and after that it was impossible to get a woman to come in, even for the day. Consequently, Fitzsimmons had not only to cook and look after the children, but to do all the packing as well. At last, however, it was all over, and the carriage stood at the door, waiting to take him and the children to the station. As he came downstairs, followed by Bobbie and Jane, someone, he fancied, called his name. He turned, and Bobbie and Jane turned too.

Bending over the balustrades of the top landing, and looking just like she had done in her lifetime, save perhaps for the excessive pallor of her cheeks, and a curious expression of fear and entreaty in her eyes, was Rosalie.

She faded away as they stared, and close beside the spot where she had stood, they saw the dim and shadowy outline of a gnarled tree.

CHAPTER VIII

THE TRUNK

A STRANGE CASE OF HAUNTING IN SYDENHAM

THE other day I went to a matinée at "The St. James's." I am fond of French Revolutionary plays, and *The Aristocrat* appealed to me, not only by reason of its picturesqueness, which is happily unimpaired by any slavish adherence to historical accuracy, but also, and mostly, perhaps, by reason of its pretty and unimpeachable sentiment. The abandoned woman — a type so many of our modern dramatists consider cannot be dispensed with — apparently did not figure in this play at all.

On this particular afternoon one of the principals happened to be away, but as the part was played to perfection by my young and charming compatriot, Miss Nina Oldfield, instead of being disappointed, I only experienced an additional pleasure. I was leaning back in my seat during the interval, thinking of Danton, Desmoulins, Marat, and other of the romantic figures of that period, when someone touched me on the shoulder and whispered, "Ghost man."

Not recognising the voice, I turned round sharply.

It was John Boulton, late dramatic critic of the *Arctus*, now a staff captain, home on leave from Egypt.

"I've just heard of a case that will interest you," he said. "It bears out two of your theories, namely, that all animals and insects have spirits, and that spirits of all kinds, when freed from the material body, can assume dimensions far exceeding —in height especially—the dimensions of the material body that they once inhabited. But come on to my Club as soon as this show is over, and I'll tell you all about it."

I accepted Boulton's invitation, and subsequently listened to the following :

"Some friends of friends of mine, the Parminters, recently took a small house in Sydenham. Now Sydenham is not in the hey-day of its popularity. Scores of the bigger houses are to let, and the smaller ones—the majority at least—have not even that air of genteel respectability which characterises houses of the same size in some of the less remote suburbs. Of course the train service is responsible for much—even to think of a twenty-five minutes' journey into Town by train, when one can go any distance on tube in next to no time, is both intolerable and demoralising. But the decay of the Palace—the Palace that twenty years ago all London flocked to see—is in itself sufficient to have generated that all-pervading atmosphere of sadness that seems to have permeated people and houses, alike, with its spirit of abandonment and desolation. However, as a set-off against the many disadvantages of Sydenham, including its high rates and dull, unattractive shops, there is its wonderful air—the purest, so many doctors say, in England. And, after all, what is of more consequence than pure air which means health ? At least, so the Parminters argued when they gave up the idea of living right in Town and bought this little two-storeyed villa close to the Crystal Palace Station.

"It had stood empty for years and was in a sad state of dilapidation ; but the owner, being on the verge of bankruptcy, had no money to lay out on it.

"'I will let you have it for a very low figure,' he had said to them, ' provided you take it as it stands.'

"The sum named was £120, and this the Parminters considered, in spite of there being a pretty stiff ground rent, a bargain price. Consequently, they closed with the offer, had the house renovated, and eventually moved in. On the day after their arrival Mrs. Parminter made a discovery. Stowed away in the loft was a long, weather-worn, bolster-shaped, brown wooden trunk, bearing on it two steamship company's labels, one marked Suez and the other London.

"There was no address on it—no name. The Parminters made inquiries of the builder who had done the repairs and of the late owner of the house, and neither could give them any clue as to the person to whom it belonged. The landlord declared that he had gone through all the rooms, including the loft, immediately before giving up the keys to Mrs. Parminter, and that he could swear that when he did so there was nothing in the house at all, no trunk of any description ; whilst the builder declared that both he and his men, when doing the repairs, had seen the trunk in the loft and had concluded that it belonged to the Parminters.

" ' Well, as nobody seems to want it, we had better keep it,' Mrs. Parminter remarked. ' I wonder what it contains ! It would be a pity to force the lock, we must get a key to fit it.'

" As no one happened to be going out just then, the trunk was pushed on one side, and the Parminters, having many other things to occupy their minds, did not give it another thought. Tired out with all the worry and work of ' moving in,' they went to bed early that night, in the room immediately beneath the loft, and fell asleep almost as soon as they had lain down. Parminter had the digestion of an ox and, never over-taxing his brain, slept, as a rule, right through the night. On this occasion, however, he awoke with a violent start to hear a strange, scraping sound on the floor overhead.

" It was just as if someone was drawing the rough edge of a stone backwards and forwards on the floor.

" This went on for some seconds ; then it abruptly ceased, and the stairs, leading from the landing outside the Parminters' room to the loft, gave a series of loud creaks. Of course stairs often creak, and one excuses their conduct on the ground of natural causes. The wood, we say, cannot expand

8

or contract, when certain changes in the temperature take place, without making some little noise, and vibration due to the passing by of some heavy vehicle must be accompanied by some slight sound. But why, I ask, do we not hear creaks in the daytime, when the traffic is more constant and changes in the temperature quite as marked? Parminter was not an imaginative man; on the contrary, he was practical to a degree. He had a hearty contempt for anything in the nature of superstition, and regarded all so-called psychists either as charlatans or lunatics. Yet, when he listened to this creaking, he was bound to admit that there was something about it that bothered and perplexed him. He got up and opened the door. There was no moon, but, on the staircase, there was a long streak of leadish blue light, that moved as Parminter stared at it, and slowly began to descend. The stairs creaked under it and, though he could see nothing beyond the light, he could hear the most peculiar rattling, scraping sound, as if some metal-clad body was in course of transit. The thing, whatever it was, at last arrived on the landing, where it remained stationary. A feeling of unutterable horror and repulsion now came over Parminter, and, springing back into the room, he shut and locked the door. The noise awoke his wife, and they both stood by the door and listened, as the creaking and rattling was renewed and the thing crossed the landing and descended the stairs into the hall. Presently there came a savage snarl, which ended in a shrill whine, that was almost human in the intensity of its agony and terror, and after that, silence.

" ' Puck ! ' Mrs. Parminter ejaculated, her teeth chattering. ' What can have happened to him ? '

" ' God knows,' Parminter replied. ' I'm not going to see.'

" They stood there shivering in their night clothes, until, from the absolute stillness of the house, they concluded that the thing had gone ; then they lighted candles and, slipping into their dressing-gowns, descended the stairs. Puck was crouching on the mat by the drawing-room door, in an attitude he often assumed when well scolded. They called him by his name. He did not answer. Then they bent over him and patted his head. Still he did not stir, and when they came to examine him more closely they discovered he was dead.

" Determined to get to the bottom of the mystery, Parminter, the following night, sprinkled the stairs all over with flour and sand. The same thing happened. First of all the scraping immediately overhead, then the creaking and rattling on the stairs, then the pause, and then the slow and stealthy descent, accompanied by the same combination of noises, into the hall. When all was still again, they examined the flour and sand. There were no imprints on it of any kind, and apparently it had not been touched, for it bore no sign whatever of anything having passed over it.

" Still Parminter would not acknowledge the

possibility of the superphysical. 'The noises we've heard,' he remarked, 'are simply the result of some curious acoustic property, not uncommon, perhaps, if we only knew it, in houses of this description. And what I saw on the stairs is, of course, merely the effect of some trick of the light which anyone who understands natural science could easily explain.'

" ' Well, all I can say is that I should like to have the whole thing explained, and to know what these natural causes that you're so fond of talking about really are,' rejoined Mrs. Parminter.

" ' So should I,' Parminter replied. ' But I can't explain it, because I'm not a scientist.'

" ' Well, get one,' was the reply. ' Get Professor Keipler.'

" Professor Keipler was the only scientist the Parminters knew. He was a German, and at that time happened to be living in Penge. At Parminter's request he came over to Sydenham and accepted an invitation to stay the night. Parminter showed him the loft, and the Professor made a very careful examination of it, pulling up one or two boards and peering into all the cracks and crevices. He tested the walls and stairs too, and admitted that he could discern nothing there that could account for some, at least, of the noises the Parminters described. When bedtime came, instead of retiring to rest, Parminter lowered all the lights, and they all three sat on the landing and waited.

" Precisely at the same time as on the ¡previous night they heard the scraping sound in the loft, then the gentle opening of a door, then a rattling of metal; and then—Parminter caught the Professor by the arm—a long, luminous something came into view. Instead, however, of descending the stairs, it mounted the wall and suddenly shot down towards them like a streak of lightning.

" Mrs. Parminter screamed, Parminter tightened his hold of the Professor, and the next thing they knew was that they were all three rolling on the floor with something huge and scaly crawling over them. It conveyed the impression that it was some gigantic, venomous, and indescribably hideous insect, furnished with many long and dreadful legs, and they shrank from its touch just as they would have shrunk from the touch of an enormous spider, black-beetle, or other creature to which they had a special aversion. The Professor had brought with him a very powerful electric torch. In the first panic it had slipped from his grasp and rolled away into the darkness, but his fingers eventually coming into contact with it, he pressed the button. In an instant the landing was flooded with light, and the thing of horror had gone. Parminter then lit the incandescent gas, and they all three went downstairs into the dining-room and had brandies and soda.

" ' Well, how do you account for it ? ' Parminter said to the Professor. ' What do you think it was ? '

"'Nothing that I can explain by any known physical law,' the Professor replied. 'I never believed in the possibility of the superphysical before, but I am convinced of it now. What struck me most about that thing, even more than its extraordinary property of completely vanishing under the influence of light, was its malignancy. Didn't you feel how intensely antagonistic it was to us?'

"'Yes,' Parminter said. 'I did.'

"'Well,' the Professor went on, 'such antagonism, such concentrated spleen and venom and bloodthirstiness—I felt the thing wanted to crush, tear, mangle, lacerate, poison me—could only originate in Hell—in a world altogether distinct from ours, where cruelty and maliciousness attain dimensions entirely beyond the scope of the physical. My advice to you is to quit the house with all haste, lest something really evil befall you.'

"Having only just moved in, and spent a lot of money on the place, the Parminters naturally did not feel inclined to carry out this advice.

"'If the place is haunted,' they argued, 'we can surely get rid of the ghost by exorcism or some other device.'

"They consulted several of their friends, and were finally persuaded to call in a priest—an Anglican, from a parish in the East End, that Mrs. Parminter used to visit when they lived in town.

"The Parminters did not tell me exactly what Father S—— did (I believe there is a special form of exorcism practised in the Church), but anyhow he could not proceed; his nerves, so he himself admitted, went all to bits, and directly the long streak of light began to crawl towards him he turned tail and fled.

"Another clerical friend whom the Parminters called in to exorcise the ghost did, I believe, complete the service; but it had no effect—the thing mounted the wall, just as it had done before, and darting downwards put the exorciser to instant flight. The Parminters next resolved to try a West End occultist. It was an expensive proceeding; but terms were at length agreed upon, and the following night the renowned psychic arrived to lay the ghost. When it was time for it to appear, this exorciser insisted upon the Parminters retiring to their room, whilst he himself remained outside on the landing alone.

"They heard him repeat a lot of gibberish, as Parminter afterwards described it to me; and then he rapped at their door and told them they need not worry any more as he had seen the ghost, the spirit of a monk, and given it the consolation it needed.

"'But why did the monk crawl and make such a queer rattling noise?' Mrs. Parminter inquired.

"'Because just before he died he lost the use of his limbs,' was the reply. 'Spirits, you know, always come back in the state they were in immediately prior to their death. The rattling was due to the fact that he wore armour; so many of the old monks combined two professions, that of soldier and priest.'

" ' But how about the speed with which the thing darted at us,' Parminter said, ' and the feeling we all had that it possessed innumerable legs ? That doesn't look much like a disabled monk, does it ? '

" ' He didn't appear like that to me,' the occultist replied. ' In all probability you had that impression because your psychic faculties are not sufficiently developed. At present you see spirits all out of focus, as it were—not in their true perspective. If you went through a proper course of training at some psychic college, you would see them just as I do.'

" ' Possibly,' Parminter said, ' but how about the gas ? I see you had it full on all the time.'

" ' That would make no difference in my case,' the occultist replied, ' because to anyone of my advanced learning ghosts can materialise in the light just as well as in the dark.'

" ' Then you feel certain the hauntings have now ceased ? ' Mrs. Parminter observed.

" ' That is what the monk told me,' was the reply ; ' and now, if you will kindly pay me my fee, I will go.'

" Parminter gave him a cheque, and he went. An hour later, when the Parminters were in bed and the house was still and dark, they heard the scraping on the floor overhead, and the thing came down. This time neither of them stirred, and the thing, as before, passed their room and descended into the hall.

" The following morning Mrs. Parminter received
a letter from her sister, Mrs. Fellowes, asking her if
she could put up the two children, Flo and Maisie,
their maid, and herself for a week. It was extremely inconvenient just then for Mrs. Parminter
to have visitors, and had it been anyone else she
would have refused ; but she was devoted to this
particular sister, and at once wrote back bidding
her come.

" The house was rather oddly constructed. On
the top story were three rooms, two quite a decent
size, but the third barely big enough for a bed, and
having two doors, one of which opened on to the
landing and the other into the loft. The loft was
very large, but so dark and badly ventilated that
it could not possibly be used for sleeping purposes.
Every room in the house being required, Mrs.
Fellowes' nursemaid, Lily, was put to sleep in the
room adjoining the loft, whilst Flo and Maisie
occupied one of the two larger rooms, and the Parminters' cook and housemaid the other. For the
first two nights after the arrival of the visitors there
were no disturbances, although Lily complained
that she had never slept worse in her life. On the
third day of their stay the children were invited out
to tea, and their mother accompanied them. When
they returned they inquired for Lily, and being told
that she had been in her room all the afternoon, they
ran upstairs to see if anything was the matter with
her.

" Maisie knocked, and receiving no reply, opened
the door and peeped in.

"Lily was lying on the bed, and on the top of her, its long antennæ waving over her face, was an enormous scaly thing with a hideous jointed body and hundreds of poisonous-looking black legs. Its appearance was so terrific, so unmistakably evil and savage, that Maisie was petrified, and stood staring at it, unable to move or utter a sound.

"Flo, wondering what had happened, peeped over her sister's shoulders, and was equally shocked. Just then someone came running upstairs, making a great noise, and the thing slowly vanished. The children then recovered the use of their tongue, and shrieked for help.

"Parminter, happening to enter the house at that moment, ran to the assistance of the children, and in a few moments the whole household was on the top landing. Lily was unconscious, and for days she was so ill that the doctor held out very little hope of her recovery. In the end, however, she pulled round, but both her throat and heart were permanently affected. Soon after this event the Parminters resold the house, as they felt they could not remain in it any longer. They had stored a good many things in the loft, and, on removing them, they came across the trunk.

"'Why, we never opened it,' Mrs. Parminter cried, trying in vain to lift up the lid.

"'No ; we were going to get a key, and then forgot all about it,' Parminter replied. 'But we'll soon remedy that. I'll send for a locksmith at once.'

" He did so, and the man, at last finding a key that fitted, opened the box.

" It was not quite empty ; on the bottom of it, stuck firmly down with two big hatpins, its long legs spread out on either side of it like a hideous fringe, was a black Indian centipede."

CHAPTER IX

THE COUGH

A CASE OF HAUNTING IN REGENCY SQUARE, BRIGHTON

I KNOW a man called Harrison. So, in all probability, do you ; so, in all probability, do most people. But it is not everyone, I 'imagine, that knows a Harrison who delights in the Christian name of Pelamon, and it is not everyone that knows a Pelamon Harrison who indulges in psychical research. Now some people think that no one unless he be a member of the Psychical Research Society can know anything of ghosts. That is a fallacy. I have met many people who, although they have had considerable experience in haunted houses, have never set a foot in Hanover Square ; and, vice versa, I have met many people who, although they have been members of the Psychical Research Society, have assured me they have never seen a ghost. Pelamon Harrison belongs to the former category. He is by vocation a gentleman undertaker, and he lives in Sussex. Some years ago, after the publication of my novel *For Satan's Sake*, which was very severely criticised in certain of the religious denominational papers, Pelamon

Harrison, championing my cause, wrote me rather an interesting letter. I went to see him, and ever since then he has not only supplied me with detailed information of all the hauntings he has come across, but he has at times sent me accounts of his own experiences. This is one of them.

Pelamon was seated in his office one day reading Poe, when the telephone at his elbow started ringing.

" Hullo ! " said Pelamon. " Who's there ? "

" Only me—Phoebe Hunt," was the reply. (Phoebe Hunt was Pelamon Harrison's housekeeper.)

" Anything the matter ? " Pelamon asked anxiously. " What is it ? "

" Oh, nothing," Mrs. Hunt replied, " only a rather queer-looking gentleman has just called and seemed most anxious to see you. He says he has been told about you by Mr. Elliot O'Donnell, and he wants you to go at once to a house in Regency Square, Brighton, No. —. He says it is very badly haunted."

" What's his name ? " Pelamon demanded.

" Nimkin," Mrs. Hunt answered, and she very carefully spelt the name—" N I M K I N."

" I'll think it over," Pelamon said, " and if I'm not home by seven o'clock, don't expect me till the morning." He then rang off, and thinking it was time he did some work, he took up his account book.

Try as he would, however, he could not keep his mind from wandering. Something kept whispering in his ear " Nimkin," and something kept telling him that his presence was urgently needed in Regency Square.

At last, unable to stand it any longer, he threw down his pen and, picking up his hat and coat, hurried off to the railway station.

At seven o'clock that evening he stood on the pavement immediately in front of No. —. Regency Square. All the blinds were down, and this circumstance, combined with an atmosphere of silence and desolation, told him that the house was no longer inhabited. Somewhat perplexed, he asked the servant next door if she could tell him where Mr. Nimkin lived.

" Not in Heaven," the girl replied tartly. " He did live in No. — till his wife died, but after that he went to live on the other side of the town. He died himself a few days ago, and I believe his funeral took place this afternoon."

" And No. — where his wife died is now empty," Pelamon observed.

" Yes, it's been empty ever since," she replied, and, sinking her voice to a whisper, "folks say it's haunted. I can't altogether bring myself to believe in ghosts—but I've heard noises," and she laughed uneasily.

" Had he any children? " Pelamon asked.

" No," the girl answered, " and he has left the money he hoarded—he was the meanest of old sticks—to the hospital for consumptives."

" A worthy cause," Pelamon commented.

The girl nodded. " His wife was a consumptive," she went on. " I remember her well—a pretty,

fair-haired creature with a lovely skin, and "—
here she shuddered—" a shocking cough." Then,
thrusting her head close to Pelamon, and fixing him
with a frightened glance, she whispered, " It was
the cough that killed her ! "

Pelamon stared at her in astonishment. " Why,
of course," he said. " It's the cough that kills all
consumptives. I've buried scores of them."

The girl shook her head. " You don't understand," she said, "but I daren't tell you any more ;
and, after all, it's only what we thought. Anyhow,
he's dead now, and a good job too. Did you want
to see him ? "

" Oh, it was nothing very particular," Pelamon
replied. " Who has the keys of the house ? "

The girl's jaws dropped and her eyes grew as big
as turtle's eggs.

" The keys ! " she exclaimed. " Mercy on us,
you don't intend going there ? "

" That's my business," Pelamon replied haughtily ;
and then, not wishing to offend her, he added : " I
heard the place was to be let, and as I want a house
in this particular locality, I thought I would call
and look at it, that's all ! I am not a burglar ! "

The girl giggled. " A burglar ! " she said. " Oh
no, you're not sharp enough for that. Besides,
the house is empty."

" What ! " Pelamon exclaimed. " Has all the
furniture been taken away ? "

" All but the blinds," the girl nodded. " There
was a sale here the day after Mrs. Nimkin was
buried, and at it crowds of people ; some of the

furniture fetched an enormous price. I did hear that the house was sold too, but I'll ask the missus to make sure."

She ran upstairs, and returned in a few minutes.

" Yes," she said, " the house is sold, and the new people are coming in soon."

" Then that settles the matter," Pelamon said, and, thanking her in his usual terse and precise way, he withdrew.

He took a brief turn on the sea front, thinking all the time of Regency Square and the mysterious individual who had interviewed Mrs. Hunt, and who must be, he thought, related to the Nimkin who had been buried that afternoon. At nine o'clock he was once again in the square. Entering the garden of No. —, he crept round to the back of the house and, finding the catch of one of the windows undone, he raised the sash and climbed in.

He had an electric torch with him, and consequently he was able to find his way about. Pelamon is very susceptible to the influence of the superphysical, and is probably far more of a psychic than the majority of those who earn their living as professional mediums. He told me afterwards that he knew No. — was haunted the moment he set his foot inside it. He could detect the presence of the superphysical both in the atmosphere and also in the shadows. Frequently in the death chambers which he had attended he had seen a certain type of shadow on the floor by the bed ; and it was this same queer kind of shadow, he said, that now crept out from the wall to meet him. But it was not the only phenomenon. From just where the shadow lay, there came a cough, a nervous, worrying cough, a regular hack, hack, hack, and when Pelamon moved, the cough and the shadow moved too. He went all over the house, into every room ; and the cough and the shadow followed him. Hack, hack, hack, he could not get rid of it. At first it merely irritated him ; but after a while he grew angry, infuriated, maddened.

"Damn you!" he yelled. "Stop it! Stop that vile, infernal hacking. Damn you! Curse you! Stop it!"

But the coughing went on, and in a hideous fit of rage, Pelamon flew at the shadow, jumped on it, stamped on it, and drawing out his clasp knife, knelt down and deliberately stabbed it. Still it went on, untiringly, ceaselessly, significantly, hack, hack, hack. Pelamon was still on the floor cutting, stabbing, blaspheming, when a taxi suddenly drew up outside the house, and the next moment the front-door bell gave a loud birr. Pelamon waited till it had rung twice ; then he answered it. A chauffeur stood on the doorstep.

"You've come to the wrong house," Pelamon said to him. "No taxi is wanted here."

"This is No. —, ain't it ? " the man ejaculated.

"Yes," Pelamon replied. "It is No. —, but that doesn't simplify matters. Who sent for you ? "

"A gentleman as lives on t'other side of the town," the chauffeur replied. "He called out to me as I was passing his house. 'Do you want a

9

job ? ' he says. ' Will you drive to No. — Regency
Square and fetch a lady and gentleman? You'll
find them there waiting for you. The gent's
name is Harrison' (Pellijohn Harrison, I think
he said, but I couldn't quite catch it). ' Never
mind the lady's. Bring 'em both here.' ''

" That's very extraordinary," Pelamon exclaimed,
" for that's my name, without a doubt. But I
don't know who the gentleman could have been,
and there's no lady here."

" Maybe there ain't no lady in the house now,"
the chauffeur said dryly, " because she's just got
in the taxi. But she was there a second or two ago.
You do like your bit of fun, don't yer ? ''

Pelamon, in a great state of bewilderment, was
about to say something, when from the direction
of the taxi came the cough, hack, hack, hack. He
knew it too well.

" There you are," the chauffeur said, with a leer.
" You must admit she's in there right enough,
and waiting till you're ready to join her."

Possessed with the feeling that he must see the
thing through, Pelamon hesitated no longer. He
got into the taxi. The coughing went on, but he
could see no lady.

They drove right through the town, and at last
stopped outside a small villa facing a church or
chapel. Concluding this must be their destination,
Pelamon got out and, bidding the chauffeur wait,
rang the front-door bell. There was no response.
He looked at the windows ; there was not a vestige
of light anywhere and the blinds were all tightly

drawn. He rang again, and rapped as well, and was about to do so a third time, when a window in the next house was raised and a voice called out : " There's no one there. There's been a funeral to-day and the house is empty."

" Whose funeral was it ? " Pelamon asked eagerly.

" Mr. Nimkin's," was the reply ; " he died last Tuesday."

" Why, what are you a-talking about ? " the chauffeur called out, descending from his perch and joining Pelamon on the doorstep. " Nimkin ! Why, that was the name of the bloke as was here less than an hour ago and told me to fetch this gentleman. No one in the house indeed, why, he's in it, and the lady that came along with this gentleman here, she's in it too. Listen to her coughing," and, as he spoke, from the other side of the closed door came the familiar sounds, hack, hack, hack.

CHAPTER X

THE SYDERSTONE HAUNTINGS

SOME years ago I published in a work entitled *Ghostly Phenomena* (Werner Laurie & Co.) an account, sent me by the late Rev. Henry Hacon, M.A., of Searly Vicarage, North Kelsey Moor, of hauntings that once occurred in the Old Syderstone Parsonage (the present Rectory has never, so I understand, been in any way disturbed). Thanks to the kindness and courtesy of Mr. E. A. Spurgin of Temple Balsall, Warwickshire (grandson of the Rev. John Spurgin), I am now able to reproduce further correspondence relative to the same case, written at the time of the occurrence—over eighty years ago.

The following paragraphs appeared in the *Norfolk Chronicle*, June 1, 1833 :—

" A REAL GHOST

" The following circumstance has been creating some agitation in the neighbourhood of Fakenham for the last few weeks.

" In Syderstone Parsonage lives the Rev. Mr. Stewart, curate, and rector of Thwaite. About six weeks since an unaccountable knocking was heard in it in the middle of the night. The family became alarmed, not being able to discover the cause. Since then it has gradually been becoming more violent, until it has now arrived at such a frightful pitch that one of the servants has left through absolute terror. The noises commence almost every morning about two, and continue until daylight. Sometimes it is a knocking, now in the ceiling overhead, now in the wall, and now directly under the feet ; sometimes it is a low moaning, which the Rev. Gentleman says reminds him very much of the moans of a soldier on being whipped ; and sometimes it is like the sounding of brass, the rattling of iron, or the clashing of earthenware or glass ; but nothing in the house is disturbed. It never speaks, but will beat to a lively tune and moan at a solemn one, especially at the morning and evening hymns. Every part of the house has been carefully examined, to see that no one could be secreted, and the doors and windows are always fastened with the greatest caution. Both the inside and outside of the house have been carefully examined during the time of the noises, which always arouse the family from their slumbers, and oblige them to get up ; but nothing has been discovered. It is heard by everyone present, and several ladies and gentlemen in the neighbourhood, who, to satisfy themselves, have remained all night with Mr. Stewart's family, have heard the same noise, and have been equally surprised and frightened. Mr. Stewart has also offered any of the tradespeople in the village an opportunity of remaining in the house and convincing themselves. The shrieking last Wednesday week was terrific. It was formerly reported in the village that the house was haunted by a Rev. Gentleman, whose name was Mantal, who died there about twenty-seven years since, and this is now generally believed to be the case. His vault, in the inside of the church, has lately been repaired, and a new stone put down. The house is adjoining the churchyard, which has added, in no inconsiderable degree, to the horror which pervades the villagers. The delusion must be very ingeniously conducted, but at this time of day scarcely anyone can be found to believe these noises proceed from any other than natural causes.

" On Wednesday se'nnight, Mr. Stewart requested several most respectable gentlemen to sit up all night—namely, the Rev. Mr. Spurgeon of Docking, the Rev. Mr. Goggs of Creake, the Rev. Mr. Lloyd of Massingham, the Rev. Mr. Titlow of Norwich, and Mr. Banks, surgeon, of Holt, and also Mrs. Spurgeon. Especial care was taken that no tricks should be played by the servants ; but, as if to give the visitors a grand treat, the noises were even louder and of longer continuance than usual. The first commencement was in the bed-chamber of Miss Stewart, and seemed like the clawing of a voracious animal after its prey. Mrs. Spurgeon was at the moment leaning against the bed-post, and the effect on all present was like a shock of electricity. The bed was on all sides clear from the wall ; but nothing was visible. Three powerful knocks were then given to the side-board, whilst the hand of Mr. Goggs was upon it. The disturber was conjured to speak, but answered only by a low hollow moaning ; but on being requested to give three knocks, it gave three most tremendous blows apparently in the wall. The noises, some of which were as loud as those of a hammer on the anvil, lasted from between eleven and twelve o'clock until near two hours after sunrise. The following is the account given by one of the gentlemen : ' We all heard distinct sounds of various kinds—from various parts of the room and the air—in the midst of us—nay, we felt the vibrations of parts of the bed as struck ; but we were quite unable to assign any possible natural cause as producing all or any part of this. We had a variety of thoughts and explanations passing in our minds *before* we were on the spot, but we left it all equally bewildered.' On another night the family collected in a room where the noise had never been heard ; the maid-servants sat sewing round a table, under the especial notice of Mrs. Stewart, and the man-servant, with his legs crossed and his hands upon his knees, under the cognisance of his master. The noise was then for the first time heard there—' above, around, beneath, confusion all '—but nothing seen, nothing disturbed, nothing felt except a vibratory agitation of the air, or a tremulous movement of the tables or what was upon them. It would be in vain to attempt to particularise all the various noises, knockings, and melancholy groanings of this mysterious something. Few nights ·pass away without its visitation, and each one brings its own variety. We have little doubt that we shall ultimately learn that this midnight disturber is but another '*Tommy Tadpole*,' but from the respectability and superior intelligence of the parties who have attempted to investigate into the secret, we are quite willing to allow to the believers in the earthly visitations of ghosts all the support which this circumstance will afford to their creed—that of *unaccountable mystery*. We understand that inquiries on the subject have been very numerous, and we believe we may even say troublesome, if not expensive."

(*Norfolk Chronicle*, June 1, 1833.)

" Syderstone Parsonage

" *To the Editor of the Norfolk Chronicle.*

" Sir,—My name having lately appeared in the *Bury Post*, as well as in your own journal, without my consent or knowledge, I doubt not you will allow me the opportunity of occupying some portion of your paper, in way of explanation.

" It is most true that, at the request of the Rev. Mr. Stewart, I was at the Parsonage at Syderstone, on the night of the 15th ult., for the purpose of investigating the cause of the several interruptions to which Mr. Stewart and his family have been subject for the last three or four months. I feel it right, therefore, to correct some of the erroneous impressions which the paragraph in question is calculated to make upon the public mind, and at the same time to state fairly the leading circumstances which transpired that night.

" At ten minutes before two in the morning, ' *knocks* ' were distinctly heard ; they continued at intervals, until after sunrise—sometimes proceeding from the bed's-head, sometimes from the side-boards of the children's bed, sometimes from a three-inch partition, separating the children's sleeping-rooms ; both sides of which partition were open to observation. On two or three occasions, also, when a definite number of blows was requested to be given, the precise number required was distinctly heard. *How* these blows were occasioned was the subject of diligent search : every object was before us, but nothing satisfactorily to account for them ; no trace of any human hand, or of mechanical power, was to be discovered. Still, I would remark, though perfectly distinct, these knocks were by no means so powerful as your paragraph represents— indeed, instead of ' *being even louder, and of longer continuance that night,* as if to give *the visitors a grand treat,*' it would seem they were neither *so* loud nor *so* frequent as they commonly had been. In several instances they were particularly gentle, and the pauses between them afforded all who were present the opportunity of exercising the most calm judgment and deliberate investigation.

" I would next notice the ' *vibrations* ' on the side-board and post of the children's beds. These were distinctly felt by myself as well as others, not only once, but frequently. They were obviously the effect of different blows, given in some way or other, upon the different parts of the beds, in several instances while those parts were actually under our hands. It is not true that '*the effect on all present was like a shock of electricity,*' but that these '*vibrations*' did take place, and that too in beds, perfectly disjointed from every wall, was obvious to our senses; though in what way they were occasioned could not be developed.

" Again—our attention was directed at different times during the night to certain sounds on the bed's-head and walls, resembling the scratchings of two or three fingers; but in *no* instance were they '*the clawing of a voracious animal after its prey.*' During the night I happened to leave the spot in which the party were assembled, and to wander in the dark to some more distant rooms in the house, occupied by no one member of the family (but where the disturbances originally arose), and there, to my astonishment, the same scratchings were to be heard.

" At another time, also, when one of Mr. Stewart's children was requested to hum a lively air, '*most scientific beatings*' to every note was distinctly heard from the bed-head; and at its close, '*four blows*' were given, louder (I think) and more rapid than any which had before occurred.

" Neither ought I to omit that, at the commencement of the noises, several feeble '*moans*' were heard. This happened more than once; after a

time they increased to a series of '*groanings*'
of a peculiarly distressing character, and proceeding
(as it seemed) from the bed of one of Mr. Stewart's
children, about ten years of age. From the tone
of voice, as well as other circumstances, my own
conviction is, that these '*moans*' could not arise
from any effort on the part of the child. Perhaps
there were others present who might have had
different impressions; but be this as it may,
towards daybreak four or six shrieks were heard—
not from any bed or wall, but as hovering in the
atmosphere in the room, where the other noises had
been principally heard. These screams were distinctly heard by *all*, but their cause was discoverable
by *none*.

" These, Sir, are the chief events which occurred at
Syderstone Parsonage on the night alluded to in your
paragraph. I understand the '*knockings*' and
'*sounds*' have varied considerably in their character on different nights, and that there have been
several nights occurring (at four distinct periods)
in which *no noises* have been heard.

" I have simply related what took place under my
own observation. You will perceive that the noises
heard by us were by no means so loud and violent
as would be .gathered from the representations
which have been made. Still, as you are aware,
they are not on that account the less real ; nor do
they, on that account, require the less rational
explanation. I trust, however, Mr. Editor, your
readers will fully understand me. I have not
related the occurrences of the night for the purpose

of leading them to any particular views, or conclusions upon a subject which, for the present at
least, is wrapt in obscurity : such is very remote from
my object. But Mr. Stewart having requested me,
as a neighbouring clergyman, to witness the incon-
veniences and interruptions to which the different
members of his family have been subject for the
last sixteen weeks, I have felt it my duty, as an
honest man (particularly among the false statements
now abroad) to bear my feeble testimony, however
inconsiderable it may be, to their actual existence
in his house ; and also since, from the very nature of
the case, it is not possible Mr. Stewart can admit
the repeated introduction of strangers to his family,
I have thought it likewise a duty I owed to the
public to place before them the circumstances which
really did take place on that occasion. In the
words of your paragraph, I can truly say : ' *I had a
variety of thoughts and explanations passing in my
mind before I was on the spot, but I left it perfectly
bewildered,*' and I must confess the perplexity
has not been diminished by the result of an investigation, which was most carefully pursued for
five days, during the past week, under the immediate
direction of Mr. Reeve, of Houghton, agent to the
Marquis of Cholmondeley, the proprietor of Syderstone and patron of the Rectory, and who, on
learning the annoyances to which Mr. Stewart was
subject, directed every practicable aid to be afforded
for the purpose of discovery. Mr. Seppings and
Mr. Savory, the two chief inhabitants of the parish,
assisted also in the investigation. A ' *trench* ' was

dug round the back part of the house, and
' borings ' were resorted to in all other parts of it
to the depth of six or seven feet, completing a
chain round the entire buildings, for the purpose of
discovering any subterranean communication with
the walls, which might possibly explain the noises
in question. Many parts of the interior of the
house, also, such as ' the walls,' ' floors,' ' false
roofs,' etc., have been minutely examined, but
nothing has been found to throw any light upon the
source of the disturbances. Indeed, I understand
the ' knockings ' within the last four days, so far
from having subsided, are become increasingly
distressing to Mr. Stewart and his family—and so
remain !—I am, Sir, your obedient servant,

" JOHN SPURGIN.

" DOCKING, June 5, 1833."

" To the Editor of the Norfolk Chronicle.

"NORWICH, June 5, 1833.

" SIR,—The detail of circumstances connected
with the Syderstone Ghost, as reported in the public
papers, is in my opinion very incorrect, and calculated to deceive the public. If the report of
noises heard on other evenings be as much ex-
aggerated as in the report of the noises which five
other gentlemen and myself heard on Wednesday

evening, the 15th of May, nothing could be better contrived to foster superstition and to aid deception. I was spending a few days with a friend in the neighbourhood of Syderstone, and was courteously invited by Mr. Stewart to sit up at the Parsonage; but I never imagined the noises I heard during the night would become a subject of general conversation in our city and county. As such is the case, and as I have been so frequently appealed to by personal friends, I hope you will afford the convenience of correcting, through the medium of your journal, some of the errors committed in the reports made of the disturbances which occurred when I was present. If the other visitors thought proper to make their statements known to the public, I have no doubt they would nearly accord with my own, as we are not, though so represented in the *Bury Post*, ' those who deal in contradictions of this sort.'

" The noises were *not loud*; certainly they were not so loud as to be heard by those ladies and gentlemen who were sitting at the time of their commencement in a bedroom only a few yards distant. The noises commenced as nearly as possible at the hour we had been prepared to expect they would—or at about half-past one o'clock a.m. It is true that knocks seemed to be given, or actually were given, on the side-board of a bed whilst Mr. Goggs' hands were upon it; but it is not true that they were ' powerful knocks.' It is also true that Mr. Goggs requested the ghost, if he could not speak, to give three knocks, and that three knocks—

gentle knocks, not ' three most tremendous blows '—
were heard as proceeding from the thin wall against
which were the beds of the children and the female
servants. I heard a scream as of a female, but I
was not alarmed ; I cannot speak *positively* as to
the origin of the scream, but I cannot deny that
such a scream may be produced by a ventriloquist.
The family are highly respectable, and I know not
any good reason for a suspicion to be excited against
any one of the members ; but as it is *possible* for
one or two members of a family to cause disturbances
to the rest, I must confess that I should be more
satisfied that there is not a connection between
the ghost and a member of the family if the noises
were distinctly heard in the rooms when *all* the
members of the family were known to be at a
distance from them. I understood from Mr.
Stewart that on one occasion the whole family—
himself, Mrs. Stewart, the children, and servants—
sat up in his bedroom during the night ; that himself
and Mrs. Stewart kept an attentive watch upon
the children and servants ; and that the noises,
though seldom or never heard before in that room,
were then heard in all parts of the room. This
fact, though not yet accounted for, is not a proof
but that some one or more of the family is able to
give full information of the cause of the noises.

   " Mr. Stewart and other gentlemen declared that
they have heard such loud and violent knocking,
and other strange noises, as certainly throw a
great mystery over the circumstance. I speak
only in reference to the knockings and the scream

which I heard when in company with the gentlemen whose names have been already made known to the public; and confining my remarks to those noises, I hesitate not to declare that I think similar noises might be caused by visible and internal agency.

"I do not deny the existence of supernatural agency, or of its occasional manifestation; but I firmly believe such a manifestation does not take place without Divine permission, and when permitted it is not for trifling purposes, nor accompanied with *trifling effects*. Now there are effects which appear to me *trifling*, connected with the noises at Syderstone, and which therefore tend to satisfy my mind that they are *not caused by supernatural agency*. On one occasion the ghost was desired to give ten knocks; he gave nine, and, as if recollecting himself that the number was not completed, he began again, and gave ten. I heard him beat time to the air of the verse of a song sung by Miss Stewart—if I mistake not, 'Home, Sweet Home'; and I heard him give three knocks in compliance with Mr. Goggs' request.

"Mr. Editor, noises are heard in Syderstone Parsonage the cause or agency of which is at present unknown to the public, but a full, a diligent investigation ought *immediately* to be made—Mr. Stewart, I believe, is willing to afford facility. If, therefore, I may express an opinion, that if two or three active and experienced police officers from Norwich were permitted to be the sole occupants in the house for a few nights, the ghost would not interrupt their slumbers, or, if he attempted to do it, they would quickly find him out, and teach him better manners for the future. The disturbances at the Parsonage House, Epworth, in 1716, in some particulars resemble those which have occurred at Syderstone, but in these days we give little credit to tales of witchcraft, or that evil spirits are permitted to indicate their displeasure at prayers being offered for the King, etc.; and therefore I hope that deceptions practised at Syderstone, if there be deceptions, will be promptly discovered, lest that parsonage become equal in repute to the one at Epworth.—I am, Sir, your humble servant,

"SAMUEL TITLOW."

(*Norfolk Chronicle,* June 8, 1833.)

SYDERSTONE PARSONAGE

"*To the Editor of the Norfolk Chronicle.*

"SIR,—Having already borne my testimony to the occurrences of the night of the 15th ult. in the Parsonage at Syderstone, and finding that *ventriloquism and other devices* are now resorted to as the probable causes of them (and that, too, under the sanction of certain statements put forth in your last week's paper), I feel myself called on to state publicly that, although a diligent observer of the different events which then took place, I witnessed

10

no one circumstance which could induce *me* to
indulge a conjecture that the *knocks, vibrations,
scratchings, groanings*, etc., which I heard, proceeded
from any member of Mr. Stewart's family, through
the medium of mechanical or other trickery :—
indeed, it would seem to me utterly impossible that
the scratchings which fell under my observation
during the night, in a remote room of the house,
could be *so* produced, as, at that time, every
member of Mr. Stewart's family was removed a
considerable distance from the spot.

"While making this declaration, I beg to state
that my only object in bearing any part in this
mysterious affair has been to investigate and to
elicit the *truth*. I have ever desired to approach
it without *prejudging* it—that is, with a mind
willing to be influenced by *facts* alone,—without
any inclination to establish either the intervention of
human agency on the one hand, or of *super-human*
agency on the other hand :—at the same time, it is
but common honesty to state that Mr. Stewart
expresses himself so fully conscious of his own
integrity towards the public that he has resolved on
suffering all the imputations and reflections which
have been or which may be cast either upon himself
or upon his family to pass without remark ; and
as he has, at different times and upon different
occasions, so fully satisfied his own mind on the
impossibility of the disturbances in question arising
from the agency of any member of his own household (and from the incessant research he has made
on this point, he himself must be the best judge),

Mr. Stewart intends declining all future interruptions of his family, by the interference of
strangers.

" Perhaps, Mr. Editor, your distant readers may
not be aware that Mr. Stewart has not been resident
at Syderstone more than fourteen months, while
mysterious noises are *now* proved to have been
heard in this house, at different intervals and in
different degrees of violence, for the last thirty years
and upwards. Most conclusive and satisfactory
affidavits on this point are now in progress, of the
completion of which you shall have notice in due
time.—I am, Sir, your obedient servant,

" JOHN SPURGIN.

" DOCKING, *June* 7, 1833."

(*Norfolk Chronicle*, June 15, 1833.)

These Declarations were inserted in the *Norfolk
Chronicle*, June 22, 1833 :—

" SYDERSTONE PARSONAGE

" For the information of the public, as well as for
the protection of the family now occupying the above
residence from the most ungenerous aspersions,
the subjoined documents have been prepared.
These documents, it was proposed, should appear
before the public as Affidavits, but a question
of law having arisen as to the authority of the

Magistrates to receive Affidavits on subjects of this nature, the Declarations hereunder furnished have been adopted in their stead. The witnesses whose testimony is afforded have been all separately examined—their statements, in every instance, have been most cheerfully afforded—and the solemn impression under which the evidence of some of them particularly has been recorded, has served to show how deeply the events in question have been fixed in their recollection. Without entering upon the question of Causes, one Fact, it is presumed, must be obvious to all (namely) That various inexplicable noises have been heard in the above residence, at different intervals, and in different degrees of violence, for many years before the present occupiers ever entered upon it : indeed, the Testimony of other respectable persons to this Fact might have been easily adduced, but it is not likely that any who are disposed to reject or question the subjoined evidence would be influenced by any additional Testimony which could be presented :—

" *Elizabeth Goff*, of Docking, in the county of Norfolk, widow, now voluntarily declareth, and is prepared at any time to confirm the same on oath, and say : That she entered into the service of the Rev. William Mantle about the month of April 1785, at which time her said master removed from Docking to the Parsonage at Syderstone, and the said Elizabeth Goff further states, that at the time of entering upon the said parsonage, two of the sleeping rooms therein were nailed up : and upon one occasion, during the six months of her continuance in the service of her said master, she well remembers the whole family were much alarmed in consequence of Mrs. Mantle's sister having either seen or heard something very unusual, in one of the sleeping rooms over the kitchen, which had greatly terrified her.—This Declaration was made and signed this 18th day of June 1833, before me, Derick Hoste, one of His Majesty's Justices of the Peace for the County of Norfolk.

" The mark (X) of Elizabeth Goff."

———

" *Elizabeth*, the wife of George *Parsons*, of Syderstone, in the county of Norfolk, blacksmith, now voluntarily declareth, and is prepared at any time to confirm the same on oath, and say : That she married about nineteen years ago, and then entered upon the occupation of the south end of the Parsonage at Syderstone, in which house she continued to reside for the space of nine years and a half. That she, the said Elizabeth Parsons, having lived at Fakenham previously to her marriage, was ignorant of the reputed circumstances of noises being heard in the said house, and continued so for about nine or ten months after entering upon it ; but that, at the end of that time, upon one occasion during the night, she remembers to have been awoke by some ' very violent and very

rapid knocks' in the lower room occupied by
them, immediately under the chamber in which
she was sleeping ; that the noise appeared to her
to be as against the stove which she supposed
must have been broken to pieces ; That she, the
said Elizabeth Parsons, awoke her husband, who
instantly heard the same noise ; that he immediately arose, struck a light, and went downstairs ;
but that, upon entering the room, he found everything perfectly safe, as they had been left upon
their going to bed ; that her husband hereupon
returned to the sleeping room, put out the light,
and went to bed ; but scarcely had he settled
himself in bed, before the same heavy blows returned ; and were heard by both of them for a
considerable time.—This being the first of the
noises she, the said Elizabeth Parsons, ever heard,
she was greatly alarmed, and requested her husband
not to go to sleep while they lasted, lest she should
die from fear ; but as to the causes of these noises,
she, the said Elizabeth Parsons, cannot, in any-
wise, account. And the said Elizabeth Parsons
further states, that about a year afterwards at
midnight, during one of her confinements, her
attention was particularly called to some strange
noises heard from the lower room. These noises
were very violent, and, as much as she remembers,
were like the opening and tossing up and down
of the sashes, the bursting of the shutters, and
the crashing of the chairs placed at the windows :
that her nurse hereupon went downstairs to
examine the state of the room, but, to the surprise

of all, found everything perfectly in order, as she had left it.—And likewise the said Elizabeth Parsons further states, that besides the occurrences hereinbefore particularly stated and which remain quite fresh in her recollection, she was, from time to time, during her residence in Syderstone Parsonage, constantly interrupted by very frightful and unusual knockings, various and irregular;—sometimes they were heard in one part of the house, and sometimes in another;—sometimes they were frequent, and sometimes two or three weeks or months or even twelve months would pass, without any knock being heard. That these knocks were usually never given till the family were all at rest at night, and she has frequently remarked, just at the time she hoped she had got rid of them, they returned to the house, with increased violence.— And finally the said Elizabeth Parsons declares, that during a residence in the Syderstone Parsonage of upwards of nine years, knocks and noises were heard by her therein, for which she was utterly unable to assign any cause.—This Declaration was made and signed this 18th day of June 1833, before me, Derick Hoste, one of His Majesty's Justices of the Peace for the County of Norfolk.

" Elizabeth Parsons."

---

[1] " *Thomas Mase*, of Syderstone, in the county of Norfolk, carpenter, now voluntarily declareth, and

is prepared at any time to confirm the same on oath, and say : That one night, about eleven years ago, while Mr. George-Parsons occupied part of the Parsonage at Syderstone, he happened to be sleeping in the attic there ; and about midnight he heard (he thinks he was awoke out of sleep) a dreadful noise, like the sudden and heavy fall of part of the chimney upon the stove in the lower sitting-room.—That the crash was so great that, although at a considerable distance from the spot, he distinctly heard the noise, not doubting the chimney had fallen and dashed the stove to pieces :—that he arose and went downstairs (it being a light summer's night) : but upon examining the state of the room and stove, he found, to his astonishment, everything as it ought to have been. And the said Thomas Mase further states, that, upon another occasion, about eight or nine years ago, while sleeping a night in Syderstone Parsonage in a room at the south end thereof, the door of which room moved particularly hard upon the floor, requiring to be lifted up in order to close or open it, and producing a particular sound in its movement, he distinctly heard all the sounds which accompanied its opening.—That he felt certain the door was opened, and arose from his bed to shut it, but, to his great surprise, he found the door closed, just as he had left it.—And finally the said Thomas Mase states, that the circumstances above related, arose from causes which he is totally at a loss to explain.—This Declaration was made and signed this 18th day of June 1833, before me,

Derick Hoste, one of His Majesty's Justices of the Peace for the County of Norfolk.

"THOMAS MASE."

"*William Ofield*, of Syderstone, in the county of Norfolk, gardener and groom, now voluntarily declareth, and is prepared at any time to confirm the same on oath, and say : That he lived in the service of the Rev. Thomas Skrimshire, about nine years ago, at which time his said master entered upon the occupation of the Parsonage at Syderstone, and that he continued with him during his residence in that place. The said William Ofield also states, that, as he did not sleep in the house, he knows but little of what took place therein during the night, but that he perfectly remembers, on one occasion, while sitting in the kitchen, he heard in the bedroom immediately over his head, a noise resembling the dragging of furniture about the room, accompanied with the fall as of some very heavy substance upon the floor.—That he is certain this noise did take place, and verily believes no one member of the family was in the room at the time.— The said William Ofield likewise states, that the noise was loud enough to alarm part of the family then sitting in the lower room, in the opposite extremity of the house ; that he is quite sure they were alarmed, inasmuch as one of the ladies immediately hastened to the kitchen to make inquiry about the noise, though his said master's family never seemed desirous of making much of these occurrences :—that he, the said Wm. Ofield, was ordered to go upstairs to see what had happened, and upon entering the room he found everything right :—he has no hesitation in declaring that this noise was not occasioned by any person in the house. The said Wm. Ofield likewise states, that, at different times during the evenings, while he was in his said master's service, he has heard other strange noises about the house, which he could never account for, particularly the rattling of glass and china in the chiffonier standing in the drawing-room, as if a cat were running in the midst of them, while he well believes no cat could be there, as the door was locked. And the said Wm. Ofield like-wise states, that he has been requested by some of the female servants of the family, who had been frightened, to search the false roof of the house, and to quiet their alarms, he has done so, but could never discover anything out of order.—This De-claration was made and signed this 18th day of June 1833, before me, Derick Hoste, one of His Majesty's Justices of the Peace for the County of Norfolk.

"WILLIAM OFIELD."

"*Elizabeth*, the wife of John *Hooks*, of Syder-stone, in the county of Norfolk, labourer, now voluntarily declareth, and is prepared at any time to confirm the same on oath, and say : That she entered the service of the Rev. Thomas Skrimshire, at Syderstone Parsonage, about seven years ago, and continued with him about four years ; that in the last year of her service with Mr. Skrimshire, about Christmas-time, while sitting by the kitchen fireside, she heard a noise resembling the moving and rattling of the chairs about the sleeping rooms immediately over her ;—that the noise was so great that one of Mr. Skrimshire's daughters came out of the drawing-room (which was removed a considerable distance from the spot in which the noise was heard) to make inquiry about it : that the manservant and part of the family immediately went upstairs, but found nothing displaced ;—and moreover that she verily believes no member of the family was upstairs at the time.—The said Elizabeth Hooks also states, that, upon another occasion, after the above event, as she was going up the attic stairs to bed, with her fellow-servant, about eleven o'clock at night, she heard three very loud and distinct knocks, as coming from the door of the false roof. These knocks were also heard by the ladies of the family, then separating for the night, who tried to persuade her it was someone knocking at the hall door. The said Elizabeth Hooks says, that although convinced it was from no person out doors, yet she opened the casement to look and, as she expected, found no one ;—indeed (being closest to the spot on which the blows were struck) she is sure they were on the door, but how and by whom given she is quite at a loss to conjecture.—

And finally the said Elizabeth Hooks states, that at another time, after she had got into her sleeping-room (the whole family besides being in bed, and she herself sitting up working at her needle) she heard noises in the passage leading to the room, like a person walking with a peculiar hop : that she was alarmed, and verily believes it was not occasioned by any member of the family.—This Declaration was made and signed this 18th day of June 1833, before me, Derick Hoste, one of His Majesty's Justices of the Peace for the County of Norfolk.

"The mark (X) of Eliz. Hooks."

———

"*Phoebe Steward*, of Syderstone, in the county of Norfolk, widow, now voluntarily declareth, and is prepared at any time to confirm the same on oath, and say : That about twenty years ago, a few days after Michaelmas, she was left in charge of Syderstone Parsonage, then occupied by Mr. Henry Crafer ; and about eight o'clock in the evening, while sitting in the kitchen, after securing all the doors, and no other person being in the house, she heard great noises in the sleeping rooms over her head, as of persons 'running out of one room into another '—' stumping about very loud ' —and that these noises continued about ten minutes or a quarter of an hour :—that she felt the more alarmed, being satisfied there was, at that time, no one but herself in the house.—And the said Phoebe Steward further states, that on Whitsun-Tuesday, eighteen years ago, she was called to attend, as nurse, on Mrs. Elizabeth Parsons, in one of her confinements, then living in Syderstone Parsonage :—That about a fortnight after that time, one night, about twelve o'clock, having just got her patient to bed, she remembers to have plainly heard the footsteps, as of someone walking from their sleeping-room door, down the stairs, step by step, to the door of the sitting-room below : —that she distinctly heard the sitting-room door open, and the chair placed near one of the windows moved ; and the shutters opened. All this the said Phoebe Steward is quite sure she distinctly heard, and thereupon immediately, on being desired, she came downstairs, in company with another female, whom she had awakened to go with her, being too much alarmed to go by herself : but on entering the room she found everything just as she had left it.—And the said Phoebe Steward further states, that about a fortnight after the last-named event, while sleeping on a bureau bedstead in one of the lower rooms in Syderstone Parsonage,—that is, in the room referred to in the last statement,—she heard ' a very surprising and frightful knock, as if it had struck the head of the bed and dashed it in pieces ' : that this knock was so violent as to be heard by Mrs. Crafer in the centre of the house :—that she, the said Phoebe Steward, and another person who was at that time sleeping with her, were very much alarmed with this heavy blow, and never knew how to account for it.   And finally, the said Phoebe Steward states, that, during the forty-five years she has been in the habit of frequenting the Syderstone Parsonage (without referring to any extraordinary statements she has heard from her sister, now dead, and others who have resided in it), that she, from her own positive experience, has no hesitation in declaring, that in that residence noises do exist which have never been attempted to be explained.—This Declaration was made and signed this 18th day of June 1833, before me, Derick Hoste, one of His Majesty's Justices of the Peace for the County of Norfolk.

" The mark (X) of Phoebe Steward."

———

" *Robert Hunter*, of Syderstone, in the county of Norfolk, shepherd, now voluntarily declareth, and is prepared at any time to confirm the same on oath, and say : That for twenty-five years he has lived in the capacity of shepherd with Mr. Thomas Seppings, and that one night in the early part of March 1832, between the hours of ten and eleven o'clock, as he was passing behind the Parsonage at Syderstone in a pathway across the glebe land near the house, when within about twelve yards of the back part of the buildings, his attention was arrested all on a sudden by some very loud ' groanings,' like those ' of a dying man—solemn and lamentable,' coming as it seemed to him from the centre of the house above :—that the said Robert

Hunter is satisfied these groans had but then just begun, otherwise he must have heard them long before he approached so near the house.—He also further states, that he was much alarmed at these groans, knowing particularly that the Parsonage at that time was wholly unoccupied, it being about a month before Mr. Stewart's family came into residence there :—that these groans made such an impression upon his mind, as he shall never lose, to his dying hour. And the said Robert Hunter likewise states, that, after stopping for a season near the house, and satisfying himself of the reality of these groans, he passed on his way, and continued to hear them as he walked, for the distance of not less than 100 yards. The said Robert Hunter knows 100 yards is a great way, yet if he had stopped and listened, he, the said Robert Hunter, doubts not he could have heard them to a still greater distance than 100 yards : ' so loud and so fearful were they, that never did he hear the like before.' —This Declaration was made and signed this 19th day of June 1833, before me, Derick Hoste, one of His Majesty's Justices of the Peace for the County of Norfolk.

" The mark (X) of Robt. Hunter."

————

" We, the undersigned chief inhabitants of the parish of Syderstone, in the county of Norfolk, do hereby certify that Elizabeth Parsons, Thomas Mase, William Ofield, Elizabeth Hooks, Phoebe

Steward, and Robert Hunter, who are now residing in this parish, and whose Declarations are hereto annexed, have been known to us for some years, and are persons of veracity and good repute.

" Witness our hands, this 18th day of June 1833.

"THOMAS SEPPINGS.

" JOHN SAVORY."

CHAPTER XI

THE GREEN VAPOUR

NEAR Bournemouth there is a house called the Caspar Beeches that never lets for any length of time. It has a very remarkable history, which, in the words of Mr. Mark Wildbridge, I now append. (Mr. Mark Wildbridge, by the way, was a clever amateur detective who died about the middle of last century, and many of his experiences, including the following, were narrated to me by one of his descendants.)

I had been attending to some newly planted shrubs in my garden, and was crossing the lawn on my way to the back premises to wash my hands, when the gate was swung open vigorously and a voice called out, " Can you tell me if Mr. Mark Wildbridge lives here ? "

I looked at the speaker. He was a tall young man, slim and clean built, obviously an athlete, a public schoolman, and very much the gentleman.

I was by no means in the mood to receive strangers, but as his type especially appeals to me, I decided to be gracious to him. " I am Mark Wildbridge," I replied. " Can I be of any service to you ? "

"Are you Mr. Wildbridge?" the young man said in astonishment. "Somehow I had formed such a different picture of you. But, of course, there is no reason why a detective should carry his trade in his face any more than an artist or author."

"Rather less reason, perhaps," I responded dryly. "Have you come to consult me professionally?"

The young man nodded. "Yes," he answered. "May I speak to you in private, somewhere where there is no chance of our being overheard?"

I conducted him to my study, and, after seeing him seated, begged him to proceed.

"Mr. Wildbridge," he began, leaning forward and eyeing me intently, "do you believe in family curses?"

"It depends," I said. "I have come across cases where there seems little doubt a family is labouring under some malign superphysical influence. But why do you ask?"

"For this reason," he replied, sitting up straight and assuming an expression of great intensity. "Two years ago I was living with my parents at the Caspar Beeches, near Bournemouth. My brother was coming home from India on sick leave, and my father and I had gone up to town to meet him, when, the day after we arrived, we got a wire to say that my mother had died suddenly. She had been absolutely well when we left her, so that the shock, as you may imagine, was terrible. Of course we hastened home at once, but the news was only too true—she was dead, and, at the inquest which followed in due course, a verdict of death from asphyxiation—cause unknown—was returned. Well, Mr. Wildbridge, exactly six months later my father was also found dead in his bedroom, and, as everything pointed to his having died in exactly the same manner as my mother, my brother and I had a detective down from Scotland Yard to inquire into the affair. He could, however, make nothing of it. The door of my father's room was found locked on the inside, the windows were all fastened, so that no one could have gained admission ; and, besides, as nothing had been touched, and not a single article was missing, there was no apparent motive for a crime. At the same time, my brother and I were far from satisfied. Although, as the detective had pointed out to us, my father was alone when he met his death, it seemed to us that his end must have been brought about by some unnatural and outside agency. The coroner's verdict was death from asphyxiation, the medical evidence tending to show that he had died from the effects of some poisonous gas. Yet whence came the gas and how was it administered ? The sanitary authorities, whom we called in, declared, after a very careful examination, that all the drains were in the most excellent repair, so we simply didn't know what to think. My brother, who had imbibed mysticism in India, at length came to the conclusion that there was some curse on us. He said that my father had on several occasions spoken very gloomily about the parents' sins being visited on their children, and I, too, had noticed that my father at times was very despondent; but I had attributed this despondency merely to moodiness, and at the time pooh-poohed my brother's suggestion that there existed a mystery—something sinister in connection with some member of our own family. But since then I have altered my opinion, for my brother, who inherited the property, has also been found dead—killed by the same diabolical agency that for some unknown reason brought about the deaths of my mother and father. The Caspar Beeches is now mine, Mr. Wildbridge, and I have come to ask you what I had better do."

" You think, of course, that you may share the fate of your mother, father, and brother ? " I asked.

" I think it extremely likely," he replied.

" You are the only one left in your family ? "

" Yes," he said, " the only one."

" And what are your plans with regard to the Caspar Beeches ? " I inquired. " Do you think of residing there ? "

" I haven't made up my mind," he replied; " that is one of the points upon which I want your advice. I want to know what you think about these deaths. Do you think they were due to some as yet undiscovered physical cause, as, for instance, some unknown disease, or some gas the sanitary authorities have not been able to trace —or, to the superphysical ? "

" I can form no opinion at present," I replied; " I must first have more details. But from what you have said, I think this case presents some novel and very extraordinary features. I should like to see the house. By the way, you haven't told me your name."

" Mansfield," the young man said—" Eldred Mansfield."

" The son of Sir Thomas Mansfield, the Bornean explorer ? "

" Yes."

" Then you are the present baronet ? "

The young man nodded.

" And in the event of your death," I remarked, " to whom do the title and estates revert ? "

" I believe to some distant relative," Sir Eldred replied. " I cannot say definitely, for I have never inquired. I have no first cousins, and I know nothing about any others."

" That is rather odd," I observed, " not to know who succeeds you. Now, tell me—of whom does your household at the Caspar Beeches consist ? "

" The butler Parry, his wife, who is house-keeper, and four other servants."

" Have the Parrys been with you long ? "

" About four years."

" Do you like them ? "

" Not altogether," Sir Eldred replied. " Parry is rather fussy and officious, and his wife much too soapy. My father, however, found them honest, and I don't suppose I could improve on them."

" Well," I said, " as I have already remarked, I can't give you an opinion till I've seen the house. Supposing you engage me as your secretary ? "

"An excellent idea," Sir Eldred cried, his face lighting with enthusiasm. "To tell the truth, I don't much like the idea of sleeping there alone. Will you go back with me to-night? I will wire to Parry to get a room ready for you."

As my time was my own just then, I agreed, and that afternoon saw me tearing off in a taxi to meet Sir Eldred at Waterloo.

The Caspar Beeches, a large old family mansion, is situated nearer Winton than Bournemouth proper, and in the midst of the most lovely forest scenery. An air of impressive sadness hung around it, which, although no doubt largely due to the season and lateness of the hour, still, I thought, owed its origin, in part, to some very different cause; and when, on entering, I glanced round the big, gloomy, oak-panelled hall with its dim, far-reaching galleries, I inwardly remarked that this might well be the home of a dozen hidden mysteries, a dozen lurking assassins, that could prowl about and hide there, without the remotest fear of discovery.

The door had been opened to us by a tall, thin, bald-headed old man, with small and rather deep-set eyes of the most pronounced blue, and a rather cut-away chin. He expressed himself overjoyed to see his young master back again, and was most emphatic in his assurances that our rooms were quite ready for us.

His wife, an elderly woman with dark, keen, penetrating eyes and slightly prominent cheek-bones, met us in the hall. I knew, of course, that she was Mrs. Parry, when she spoke, but her voice came as a surprise. In striking contrast to her appearance it was soft and low, and not altogether unmusical. The other servants did not interest me much—they were the type one sees in all well-to-do establishments—and yet I felt that if I were to get at the bottom of the mystery that unquestionably shrouded the deaths of Sir Eldred's three relatives, I must watch everyone very closely ; for the key to a great secret is often found where least expected.

We dined at eight o'clock, and after dinner I took a brief survey of the house. This enabled me to form some idea of the general arrangement of the rooms and where certain of them were situated. My bedroom, I found, was separated from that of Sir Eldred by the entire length of a corridor, and at my suggestion the room adjoining his own was allotted to me instead. Mrs. Parry demurred a little at the change, remarking that the room next Sir Eldred's had not been aired ; but I told her I was not in the least degree likely to catch cold, as I had often slept in queer places, having spent a considerable portion of my life in the backwoods of Canada. Sir Eldred laughed.

" You don't know what care we are taken of here," he said. " I can assure you, if I were to feel even the suspicion of a draught it would be considered a most terrible calamity."

" Yes, indeed," Mrs. Parry said, with a sigh, " after what has happened, Sir Eldred's life is so precious we feel we cannot be too careful."

" Have you any idea what killed your late master and mistress ? " I asked her aside. " What terrible times you have gone through ! "

" Ay, terrible indeed," she said. " A kinder master and mistress no one could have had. Parry and I always thought something blew in from outside. There is too much vegetation in the grounds, and it grows so near the house. They do say the place is built on the site of a morass."

" A morass, and in Hampshire ! " I laughed. " Why, that sounds incredible. The soil is surely gravel."

" So it may be—now," she replied. " I'm speaking of many years ago. The house is very ancient, sir."

I asked Sir Eldred afterwards if there was any truth in her remark, and he said, " Yes, I believe there was a swamp here once; at least there is mention of one in a very old history of Hampshire that we have in the library. It was drawn off towards the end of the sixteenth century when the house was built. But I'm surprised at the Parrys knowing anything about it, for I've never heard anyone allude to it—not even my father."

" Are the Parrys of the ordinary servant class ? " I asked.

" I believe so," Sir Eldred replied; " but I really know nothing of their antecedents, for I seldom encourage them to speak. As I told you, they both rather get on my nerves."

That night, some hours after the household had retired to rest, I took a rope out of my portmanteau, and, fixing one end of it securely to the bedstead, lowered myself out of the window on to the ground beneath. Then, keeping under cover of the pine trees, and evading the moonbeams as much as possible, I made a detour of the house. The night air smelt pure and sweet. Heavily charged with the scent of pinewood and heather, there was absolutely nothing about it even remotely suggestive of poisonous gas.

As I was about to emerge from the trees to re-enter the house, I heard a slight crunching sound on the gravel. I sprang back again into the gloom, and as I did so, two figures—a man and girl—stole noiselessly past me.

The girl I could not see distinctly, as her head was partly enveloped in a cloak, but the face of the man stood out very plainly in the moonlight—it was the face of a black!

What could a black man and a young girl be doing prowling about the grounds of the Caspar Beeches at that hour of night ? Who were they ?

I did not say a word to anyone, but the following night—at the same hour—I again hid amongst the trees, and the same figures passed me. Then I stole out of my lair and followed them.

On quitting the premises they took the high road to Bournemouth, and finally entered a house in the Holdenhurst Road. Making a mental note of the number of the house, I retraced my steps homeward, and early the next morning I sent the following telegram to Vane, who often accompanies me on my expeditions, and to whose quick wits I owe much :

" Have an important case on hand. Meet me this evening entrance to Bournemouth pier 7 p.m."

After dispatching this telegram I returned to the Beeches, and asked Sir Eldred to show me the rooms in which the three deaths had taken place. I then examined these rooms most minutely, but I could discover nothing in them that could in any way help me to form a theory or even get a suggestion.

" When were the deaths first discovered ? " I asked.

" Not until the morning," Sir Eldred replied, " when the servants, getting no reply to their knocks, became alarmed, and eventually the doors were forced open."

" And in each case death had taken place in bed ? "

" Yes."

" Did you have the same doctor to all three of your relatives after their deaths had been discovered ? " I asked Sir Eldred.

" Yes," he said. " Dr. Bowles. He has attended us for years."

" What age is he ? " I inquired.

Sir Eldred thought a moment. " About sixty-four or five," he replied. " He attended my father long before he was married."

" Then he would be a little old-fashioned," I said. " He might not, for instance, have much knowledge of the newest poisons. New poisons, you know, both in the form of liquid and gases, are constantly being discovered. Many are imported from Germany and the East. Might I see Dr. Bowles ? "

" Certainly," Sir Eldred replied; " but I fear he cannot help you much, as all he knew he made public at the inquests."

Sir Eldred was right practically. In my interview with Dr. Bowles, I found that he could tell me little beyond what I already knew. " Can you," I asked him, " describe the appearance of the bodies and the effect on them of the gas which you say, in all probability, caused the asphyxiation ? Was there anything specially remarkable in the facial contractions or colour of the skin ? "

" Yes," he said, " there was an infinite horror, such horror as I have never seen in human faces before," and he shuddered as he spoke. Then he gave me a minute description of the bodies, which I took down in my notebook and posted to a specialist in Oriental poisons whom I knew in London.

" Was there nothing else in the three cases that struck you as unusual ? " I asked Dr. Bowles. " No peculiarity in common ? "

He thought for a moment, and then said, "Nothing beyond the fact that all three died precisely at the same time—ten minutes past two in the morning."

" The time when human vitality is at the lowest, and superphysical phenomena the most common Were the victims in a normal state of health ? Was there any family or hereditary disease ? "

" Yes, valvular weakness of the heart."

" Which would render them more susceptible to the influence of poison ? "

" Poison and shock. The inhalation of certain poisons has a particularly deadly effect on people suffering from cardiac defection."

" Could the poison have been self-inflicted ? Are people suffering with such a disease prone to suicide ? "

" Only, as a rule, when the disease is in a very advanced state—you then get delirium, hallucinations, and morbid impulses."

" And none of these symptoms were noticeable in the deceased ? "

" Not in a sufficiently marked degree to warrant the suggestion of suicide."

" Have you no theory ? "

The doctor shook his head. " None whatever," he said; " and yet I'm sorry to say I can't help feeling there is something very sinister about it all— something that bodes ill for Sir Eldred."

Much disappointed, I returned to the Caspar Beeches, and was making another inspection of the room in which one of the tragedies had occurred when, chancing to glance at the mirror over the mantelshelf, I caught the reflection of a pair of dark eyes fixed inquiringly at me. I looked round, and a figure passed along the passage. It was Mrs. Parry. She had evidently been peeping at me through the slightly open door, which I could have sworn I had closed. This made me careful. If I meant to unravel this mystery, I must on no account be seen doing anything that might arouse suspicion as to my real identity. Hence I determined to confine myself more to the study in future, and the rest of the morning I spent taking down in short-hand letters which Sir Eldred dictated. Walls have ears, and the sound of Sir Eldred dictating to me, I argued, might prove convincing.

A week passed and I discovered nothing. There was nothing in the demeanour of any of the servants to give me the slightest reason for suspecting them ; if any of them were " in the know " they kept their secret absolutely to themselves. At night, as soon as I deemed it safe, I slipped on a pair of rubber shoes and crept about the house and grounds, but with no result. On the morning of the eighth day I received two letters—one from Vane, who had taken furnished apartments next door to the house I had noted in the Holdenhurst Road, and the other from Craddock, the poison specialist.

" I have at last found out something about those two people," Vane wrote. " They call themselves Effie and George Tyson. Tyson is an assumed name ; the girl is the daughter of Parry, Sir Eldred's butler, and the man is Henry Mansfield, nephew of Sir Thomas."

" Great heavens ! " I could not help exclaiming. " This is news indeed. Sir Eldred assured me that he had no very near relatives."

" Their bedroom is only separated from mine," the letter went on, " by a very thin wall, and when I had removed a brick I could catch every word they said. There's some mystery, and I'm going to try and solve it for you.   Watch at the Beeches. I believe there is something extra in the wind. Effie has been there already this morning, and she and George are both going there again late this evening."

The other letter, from Craddock, was as follows :

" There's only one gas that produces all the effects you describe," he said, " and that has certainly been hitherto unknown in England; indeed, the knowledge of it has been strictly confined to one region—a district in the south-east of Borneo. The natives there worship a great spirit, which they name the Arlakoo or Hell-faced one, and they never invoke it save when they desire the death of a criminal, or some very aged, useless member of the tribe.   They then prepare a mixture of herbs and berries, which they first of all dry, and, at the psychical hour of two in the morning, put in an iron pot and take into the presence of their intended victim.   Then, having set fire to the preparation, which, though rather difficult to ignite, burns slowly and surely when once aflame, they close all the openings of the hut or room and beat a precipitate retreat.   A few minutes later the spirit they have invoked appears, and, simultaneous with its materialisation, the mixture burns a bright green and emits a peculiarly offensive gas.   The result is invariably death: the shock produced by the harrowing appearance of the apparition, coupled with the poisonous nature of the fumes, is more than the human mechanism can stand.   Of course all this would be mere moonshine to anyone who is un-initiated in Eastern ways and doesn't believe in ghosts. The Bournemouth doctors would pooh-pooh it altogether. There is no other gas that I know of that produces the effects you have described. If there is another case, let me know, as I should much like to see the victim."

A ghost! A ghost employed for the purpose of murdering someone! Even to me, confirmed believer in the Unknown as I am, the idea seemed wildly improbable and fantastic. And yet, what else could have produced that look of horror in the faces? What else could have killed them?

That evening, Sir Eldred and I sat in the smoke-room after dinner and chatted away as usual. We had our coffee brought to us at nine o'clock, and at ten-thirty we retired to bed. Sir Eldred had appeared fidgety and nervous all the evening, and, as we were ascending the stairs, he asked me if I would mind sitting up with him.

" I feel I shan't sleep to-night," he said, " as I've got one of my restless moods on. If it won't be tiring you too much, will you come and sit with me ? "

I said I would with pleasure, but I did not join him at once, as I wanted the servants to think we had gone to our respective rooms and to bed as usual. I also wanted whatever there might be in the wind to mature.

On entering my room, I opened the window with as little noise as possible, and was on the verge of lowering myself into the garden when I espied someone among the trees. I was going to draw back, when the figure signalled, and I at once knew it was Vane.

Another minute and I had found him. " He's here," he whispered, " be on the qui vive, and if you want help call. See, I'm armed." And he pointed significantly to his breast pocket. He was going to say something else when we heard steps— soft, surreptitious steps that hardly sounded human —coming in our direction. I immediately withdrew to the house and hastened to Sir Eldred. At my suggestion we both sat by the window, which I noticed was shut—Sir Eldred, I knew, was very susceptible to the cold—and I arranged the curtains so that we could not be seen from the outside. Sir Eldred occupied a sofa and I an easy chair. For some time we talked in low voices, and then Sir Eldred grew more and more drowsy till he finally fell asleep.

It was one of the most exquisite nights I had ever seen—the moon, so full and silvery, and everywhere so calm, so gentle, and so still. Not a breath of air, not a leaf stirring, not a sound to be heard ; nothing save the occasional burr of a great black bat as it hurled itself past the window and went wheeling and skimming in and out the tall, slender pines. I sat still, my eyes wandering alternately from the window to Sir Eldred. Whence would come the danger my instinct told me threatened him ? How calmly he slept ! How marked and handsome were his boyish features !

Suddenly from afar off a distant church clock began to strike two, each chime falling with an extraordinary distinctness on the preternatural hush.

Hardly had the last reverberating echoes ceased before there was a loud click from somewhere near the fireplace, and the next moment came a faint smell of burning. Then I confess—remembering all Craddock had told me—I was afraid. Everything in the room—the big, open fireplace, the dark, gleaming wardrobe, the quaintly carved chairs, the rich but fantastically patterned curtains, the sofa, and even Sir Eldred himself—I hardly dared look at him—seemed impregnated with a strange and startling uncanniness. The green light! Was this the prelude to it? Was the terrible Bornean phantasm getting ready to manifest itself?

I struggled hard, and, at last, overcoming the feeling of utter helplessness that had begun to steal over me, rushed to the windows. Frantically throwing them open, I was preparing to do the same to the door, when a low, ominous wail, sounding at first from very far away, and then all of a sudden from quite close at hand, brought me to a standstill, and the whole room suddenly became illuminated with a glow, of a shade and intensity of green I have never seen before. Again there came an awful struggle. I felt eyes glaring at me, eyes that belonged to something of infinite hideousness and hate, to something that was concentrating its very hardest to make—to force—me to look; and it was only by an effort that smothered my chest and forehead

in beads of cold sweat I desisted. Groping my
way across the room, with my eyes tightly closed,
I eventually reached the sofa. Thank God! Sir
Eldred was still asleep. Tired with a day's hard
exercise, he had fallen into the soundest of
slumbers. Putting one hand over his eyes, and
seizing him by the shoulder with the other, I
speedily roused him. " Quick, quick! " I shouted.
" For the love of God get up quick! Keep your
mouth tightly shut and follow me." Pushing and
dragging him along, I made for the direction of the
door. The poison fumes now began to take effect ;
my temples throbbed, my brain was on fire, a tight,
agonising feeling of suffocation gripped my chest
and throat, and, as I staggered with Sir Eldred
across the threshold on to the landing beyond, a
sea of blackness suddenly enveloped me, and I
knew no more.

.   .   .   .

On coming to, I found myself lying on the floor
of the corridor with Vane bending over me. " I
was just in time," he said. " I saw you at the
window, saw you suddenly throw up your arms
and stagger away from it, and, guessing what was
happening, I ran to the house and, climbing up
the rope you had left hanging out of your window,
I managed to reach you."

" Sir Eldred ? " I panted.

" Oh, he's all right," Vane replied. " He wasn't
really so far gone as you. A few minutes more,
though, and you would both have been dead.
Now keep cool and don't say anything about it.

As soon as the air has cleared—quite cleared mind—go to bed, and come down in the morning as if nothing had happened. Fortunately you made no noise, and I feel sure no one saw me enter the house. If you will let me take the lead in this affair, I think we may ferret the whole thing out. But we must go carefully. You don't mind my playing the part of instructor ? "

" No," I laughed, " I don't mind how despotic you are so long as we get to the bottom of this mystery. Fire ahead."

" Very well then," Vane said. " Get up now and hurry off to bed. And remember—both of you—not a word to anyone."

Vaulting on to the window-sill as he spoke, he caught hold of the rope and was speedily lost to view.

When we came down in the morning we were very careful to make no allusion to the night's happening before the servants, but strove to appear quite normal and unconcerned.

I watched Parry's face when he first encountered us, but it was quite immobile. " He is either quite innocent," I thought, " or a very old hand."

When we were alone, Sir Eldred was very anxious to hear what I thought. " Have you been able to form any theory," he asked, " because I haven't. I don't see how any of the servants could have let that infernal stuff loose in the room last night. I can swear there was no one there but ourselves. And for the life of me I can't see any motive. If any living person is responsible for it, he must be a lunatic, for no one here has anything to gain by my death."

" You are quite sure you have no near relatives ? " I said.

" Absolutely," he replied. " To the best of my knowledge I am the very last of the Hampshire Mansfields."

Our conversation was abruptly ended by the entrance of a maid with a sealed note. It was from Vane.

" At eleven o'clock to-night," he wrote, " get Sir Eldred to tell the Parrys they must sit up with him and you in his bedroom. See that he doesn't let them off, as they are sure to make excuses. Also get Craddock to come down by an early afternoon train, and tell him to call round and see me immediately he arrives. Leave the rest to me."

This note needing no reply, I hastened off at once to the General Post Office and telegraphed to Craddock. Fortunately he was at home, and wired that he would leave Waterloo by the two o'clock train. The remainder of the day passed very slowly. At ten o'clock that night someone whistled from the pines, and I knew at once that it was Vane. Craddock was with him. I conducted them both into Sir Eldred's room, where they were closeted together for some time, neither Sir Eldred nor I being allowed to enter. At last eleven o'clock arrived, and Sir Eldred went to fetch the Parrys. Both strongly demurred. Parry declared he was

unwell, and Mrs. Parry said she had never heard
of such a thing; but Sir Eldred insisted, and they
were obliged at last to follow him upstairs. Vane
and Craddock had hidden themselves so that the
Parrys only saw me.

" What do you want us to do ? " Parry asked
nervously.

" Merely to sit up with us and watch," Sir Eldred
said. " Mr. Anderson " (my alias) " and I have a
presentiment that something may happen to-night
and we don't relish the idea of facing it alone."

" I'd really rather not, sir," Parry faltered.

" That doesn't matter," Sir Eldred said sternly.
" It is my wish. Come, if you talk like that, I
shall begin to think you are both afraid. We will
arrange ourselves round the fireplace. I've an
idea that whatever comes will come down the
chimney. You sit there, Parry, next to Mr. Anderson. Mrs. Parry shall sit by me." And without
further to do he pushed them both into their seats.
I could see they were very much agitated, but they
both lapsed into silence, and for some considerable
time no one in the room spoke. My thoughts, as
I presumed did Sir Eldred's, chiefly centred round
the question as to what was the great surprise
Vane had in store for us. What he discovered ? What had he been so carefully plotting
with Craddock ?

On flew the minutes, and at last Sir Eldred struck
a match; for the moon was temporarily hidden
by big, black, scouring clouds. " Egad ! " he
said, " It's close on two. The hour fatal to my

family. If anything is going to happen to-night it should take place almost immediately."

" If I was you, sir," Mrs. Parry burst out, " I wouldn't sit up any longer. I feel sure nothing will happen to-night, and if it does, our being here can do no good."

" That's the truth," Parry echoed.

" You must wait a little longer," Sir Eldred said. " See, it's almost on the stroke ! " As he spoke, the moon shone out again in all her brilliant lustre, and every object in the room became clearly visible. Every eye was fixed on the clock.

" I'm going," Mrs. Parry cried, springing to her feet. " I'm going, Sir Eldred, if you give me notice to leave. I've had enough of this nonsense." She was about to add more, when there was a sudden click, exactly similar to the click we had heard the preceding night, the dome-shaped top of the clock flew open, and the smell of something burning, but a far sweeter and more subtle odour than that of the night before, filled the room. In an instant the whole place was in an uproar. Mrs. Parry shrieked for help, and declared she was being choked, whilst Parry, falling on his knees, clutched hold of Sir Eldred and implored his forgiveness.

" Now I'm about to die, sir," he whined, " I'll confess all. It's that cousin of yours, George, who you never heard tell of. He's married to my daughter Effie, and he wanted to come into your property. He put us up to it ; we only acted at his bidding."

" That's a lie," a voice called out, and from

behind the window-curtain stepped Vane, closely followed by Craddock. " You see, you can't help lying, Parry, even when death stares you in the face. Open the window a little wider, Mr. Craddock, so that all this smoke, which is quite harmless, by the way, can get out, and I'll explain everything. The two people who have been in the habit of prowling about your premises at night, Sir Eldred, are Effie, the daughter of these miscreants here, and George Mansfield, the son of your Uncle Richard, whom Parry, truthful for once in his life, said you had never heard of. Your father never mentioned his nephew to you because he was a half-caste, Richard Mansfield, to your father's undying disgust, having married a native of Borneo. George was brought up in Borneo, and only came to England for the first time three years ago, shortly after his father's death. He had heard all about the family quarrel, and, arriving in this country with none too friendly feelings towards your parents, sought an interview with Sir Thomas, who, if George's version of it is correct, was very curt, forbidding him ever again to enter the house. Filled with intense hatred against you all, George Mansfield went to London, and about that time met Effie Parry, who was then on ' the halls,' acting under the name of Grahame. In due course of time he married her, and it was she who first suggested to him the idea of contriving by some means or other to come into the family estate. It is easy enough to gather what lay at the back of her brain when she used the euphemism

' some means or other.' Life in the south-eastern states of Borneo, from which George Mansfield hails, is held of small account ; he at once tumbled to the suggestion, and decided to summon to his assistance a spirit they worship out there called Arlakoo. In order to invoke the Arlakoo it was essential that certain herbs should be procured, and this necessitated time and expense. Eventually, however, through the agency of friends—Borneans— they were obtained. Then came the question of introducing them into the right quarters. Effie's parents both inherit criminal tendencies : Parry's Uncle James was a notorious forger, and Mrs. Parry's grandmother was hanged for baby-farming. You needn't look so indignant, you two, for I've been to the C.I.D.—you know what the C.I.D. is— for my information. Well, the Parrys were taken into confidence, and Sir Thomas, being in need of both a butler and housekeeper just then, the two applied for the posts and got them. The rest was comparatively easy. George is an engineer by profession and has a good inventive faculty. Coming to this house when the family were all away, he espied the clock you see on the mantelshelf, in the room your mother and father slept in, and, on examining the dome, discovered that it opened, and that there was a Cupid inside it which, when in proper working order, bounced out whenever the hour struck. It appears to have been in your family a good many years, Sir Eldred, for George Mansfield had previously come across a reference to it in one of his father's diaries, and his fertile brain now conceived the idea of using it in the process of carrying his scheme into effect. In the place of the Cupid he resolved to insert a miniature brazier containing the herbs and supplied with an electric fuse, the mechanism of which could be so contrived that whenever the clock should strike two, and two only, the dome would fly open, the brazier spring up, and the herbal preparation be ignited. He was only too well aware of the hereditary tendency of the Mansfield family to heart disease, and calculated that the shock of seeing so awful an apparition as the Arlakoo (which he firmly believed he could call up), together with the poisonous fumes that accompanied it—provided the door and windows were shut, which could be accomplished with the assistance of the Parrys—would encompass the deaths he desired. He chose, for his first victim, your mother. The day you and your father went to London to meet your brother, Parry smuggled George Mansfield into the house, and the latter, seizing an opportunity when your mother was out, fitted up the clock with the brazier containing the herbal preparation and the fuse. As you know, his diabolical scheme succeeded only too well, not only your mother, but your father and brother falling victims to it. This morning Mrs. Parry paid a visit to her son-in-law, and I overheard their conversation. Great surprise was expressed at the failure of the clock yesterday, and it was decided to try it again to-night. This is the result. The vapour you saw come out of the clock just now was a quite harmless gas which Mr. Craddock substituted for the original preparation George Mansfield had put there. We caught George nicely in the garden shortly after nine. We threatened to treat him in a thoroughly Bornean fashion "— and Vane produced his revolver—" and he then confessed everything. He is now in the safe custody of the C.I.D. men."

" How did you come to suspect the clock, Vane ? " I asked.

" You forget the hole in the wall," he said, laughing. " I overheard continual allusion to the clock, and ' filling and charging ' it again, and as I knew it was not customary to fill and charge clocks, I at once smelt a rat. My suspicions were confirmed when I came to your rescue last night and saw tiny spirals of the green vapour still emanating from the dome-shaped top. I consulted with Mr. Craddock, and with his assistance I was able to carry out this little plot which, I think, we will all agree has succeeded almost beyond expectation. Any more questions ? "

" Not for the present, Mr. Vane," Sir Eldred said. " I must, first of all, express my deep sense of gratitude to you for the clever way in which you have managed to frustrate the plot to take my life. You have captured one villain ; it now remains to deal with these scoundrels here. I wish to goodness my cousin had not been involved in it. I suppose, by the way, there is no doubt that this George Mansfield is my cousin ? "

" I fear none whatever," Vane said. " I called at his rooms when I knew he was out, and found documents there which fully established his identity. I'm afraid you must prosecute him with the others."

But Sir Eldred, fortunately, was spared that degradation ; for hardly had Vane finished speaking when one of the C.I.D. men arrived at the house and informed us that George Mansfield was no more. He had evaded justice by swallowing a poisonous lozenge which he had secreted in his handkerchief.

The Parrys were let go ; the law does not acknowledge the superphysical, and Sir Eldred recognised the futility of prosecuting them. They eventually went to Canada and were heard of no more. The Caspar Beeches, however, had got a sinister name ; no tradespeople would venture within its grounds after dusk, and no servants would stay there. Sir Eldred himself lived in a constant state of fear, and confided in me that he frequently heard strange noises—doors opening and shutting of their own accord, and soft, inexplicable footsteps. Eventually the house was shut up, and, although it has since been periodically occupied, no one ever cares to remain in it for long.

When once invoked, it seems that spirits, especially evil ones, have an unpleasant habit of clinging to a person or place, and, in spite of what some people assert, can seldom, if ever, be laid.

CHAPTER XII

THE STEPPING-STONES

BETWEEN Coalbrookdale and the Wrekin, in a charmingly wooded valley, flows a stream crossed by seven stepping-stones, and on one bank of the stream are the ruins of what was once a farmhouse. People shun the spot at night, and tell strange tales of the uncanny things that are seen there.

The following narrative may very possibly afford an explanation of the alleged hauntings.

About noon one stifling hot day in August, rather more than thirty years ago, Robert Redblake Casson, senior partner of the firm of Casson, Hunter & Co., ivory merchants, of Old Queen Street, London, walked into the Fox and Greyhound Inn, Coalbrookdale, and ordered luncheon. While he was eating—there was no one else in the dining-room at the time—his eyes wandered to a large oil-painting hanging on the wall facing him. It represented a stream spanned by seven large stepping-stones. In the background of the picture, and leading to the bank of the stream, was a broad and very white pathway, bordered on either side by a thickly planted row of lofty pines. The artist, Casson thought, had depicted this scene with a more than ordinary touch of realism. The trees were no mere paint-and-canvas duds, but things of life—things that stood out prominently, each with an individuality of its own. He could almost see them move, see the rustling of their foliage and hear the creaking of their gently swaying bodies. Their shadows, too, were no empty, meaningless daubs, such as one too often sees in pictures, but counterparts, living, breathing counterparts, that, while conveying a sense of the physical, conveyed also a suggestion of the inexplicable. As to the water in the stream which rippled and babbled as it flowed, Casson could feel the speed and gauge the shallowness of it everywhere, saving round the centre stepping-stone, where it was green, and seemed to possess the stillness that great depths alone can generate. There was sunlight everywhere on the surface of the water, and here and there it shone and sparkled with all the brilliant lustre of the goldfishes' scales ; but despite this animation, a sense of utter loneliness, a feeling of intense isolation, seemed to permeate the whole thing, and Casson, as he gazed, felt both chilled and depressed.

He was still looking at the picture, and wondering what there could be in it to cause such a sensation of chilliness, when something made him glance at the stepping-stones, and, to his utter amazement, he saw the centre one suddenly begin to oscillate.

Thinking it must be some kind of optical illusion, Casson rubbed his eyes and looked again, but the stone was still shaking, and he fancied he could discern the shadowy and indistinct outline of something or someone standing on it, swaying violently to and fro.

The phenomenon lasted some seconds, and then very abruptly ceased.

Casson got up from the table and walked right up to the picture. He examined it closely, and, oddly enough, although he was standing on the floor a foot or so away from the canvas, he yet felt he was absorbed by it, and part and parcel of the surroundings it depicted. The stone was quite motionless now, but despite this fact, the fact that it now lay firmly embedded in its cup-like basin, Casson was acutely conscious that it had moved. Moreover, its present stillness was of the most impressive nature; it was, as it were, the stillness that only comes after great emotion. Casson looked for the name of the artist, and at last, in one corner of the canvas, painted in sepia to tone with the general colouring, he found the signature. It was " Ralph L. Wotherall."

" Good heavens ! " he ejaculated ; " this must be my old friend. There cannot be two Ralph L. Wotheralls. Besides, I remember he used to be fond of painting, and, judging from this specimen, he must have taken to it professionally. How I should like to meet him again ! "

His memory ran back a clear score of years. He and Wotherall had been the staunchest of friends ; they had shared a study in Dempster's House at Harley. Wotherall was quite the best boy in the school in drawing ; indeed, it was about the only subject he was good in; and he had often remarked to Casson that whatever his father, who was a big timber merchant, might desire to the contrary, he meant to go to the Slade School in London and be an artist. He decorated the walls of the study with sketches and caricatures of the boys and masters—Casson even now laughed as he thought of some of them—and during his last term at the old place he had executed an oil-painting. If Casson remembered correctly, it depicted a river (Wotherall had always evinced a very strong fascination for water scenery), and was hung in a very conspicuous place over the mantelpiece.

Wotherall had not been popular at Harley. He was no good at games, and did not take the trouble to conceal his dislike of them. Besides, he had no respect for conventions; he did not have a fag, and inveighed hotly against those who did; he thought nothing of the " caps " and other big-wigs, and was invariably in trouble, either with a master, a House Sixth, or somebody of an equally recognised importance. Still, for all that, he had been a most excellent chum, and he, Casson, had repeatedly felt a longing to see him again, if only to chat about the many escapades they had had together. What had become of him, he wondered? Strange that that stone in the picture should have attracted his attention—should have led him to look for the name of the artist, and to discover in it his old friend! Of course the rocking of the stone was a hallucination. Probably his sight had played him a trick or his brain had suddenly become giddy.

How could a stone in a picture—a thing of mere paint and canvas—suddenly start rocking? The thing was too fantastic for words, and he walked back to his seat, laughing. Ringing the bell, he asked to see the landlord, and when the latter appeared, he inquired of him how he had come by the picture, and if he knew the artist.

" I bought that picture, sir," the landlord replied, " of a woman of the name of Griffiths. I happened to be passing her house—Stepping-Stone Farm, they call it—one day, when she was having a sale of some of her live stock, together with a few odds and ends in the way of surplus furniture, books, pictures, etc. I am very fond of a good landscape, sir, particularly with a bit of water in it, and there was something about this one that specially appealed to me. That, sir, is the stream that flows outside the old woman's house, and it was painted, so she informed me, by an artist who used to lodge with her, but had to leave in the end because he was stony-broke, and hadn't the where-withal to go on paying the rent. A not uncommon happening with artists, sir, so I have always been given to understand. From what I gathered he owed the old woman pounds, and the few things he left behind him—knick-knacks and a couple of pictures—I bought the lot—was all the compensation she could ever get out of him."

" You don't know where he went, I suppose ? " Casson said.

" No," the landlord replied, shaking his head. " Mrs. Griffiths did not volunteer that information, and, as I was not particularly interested in the fellow, I didn't ask her. She doesn't live very far from here, however, and if you would like to see her, sir, you could hire a trap and drive over, or even walk—though, maybe, you'd find walking a bit too tiring this weather."

Casson thanked the landlord, and, feeling particularly fit and well, decided to set off at once on foot to Stepping-Stone Farm. He had little difficulty in finding the way, thanks to the prodigality of the local authorities in their distribution of signposts, and the sun had hardly begun to set, when a sudden swerve of the road showed him an avenue of trees that he instantly identified as that depicted in Wotherall's picture. Everywhere he encountered the same atmosphere of intense loneliness and isolation, not untinged with a melancholy, that had the most depressing effect, and filled his mind with a hundred and one dismal reflections.

Advancing over the white soil he soon heard the rushing of water, and saw, straight ahead of him and apparently barring his progress, a broad stream, that seemed unusually full of water for the time of year. As he drew near he perceived the stream was spanned by seven stepping-stones, and, drawing nearer still, he saw that, just as in Wotherall's picture, the water on either side the middle and largest of the stones formed two big pools, one of which was singularly green and suggestive of very great depth.

On the opposite side of the stream, almost on

its very bank, a farmyard encircled a long, low building, the walls of which were barely visible beneath a profusion of pink and white roses, clematis and honeysuckle. Casson thought he had never seen anything quite so enchanting, and, being a man who invariably acted upon impulse, decided to ask Mrs. Griffiths, whose house it undoubtedly was, to put him up for the night. To do that, however, he would of course have to cross the stream. Now Casson had often crossed deep rivers in Norway by stepping-stones, and in crossing these rivers he had twice seen a man slip and, with one agonising shriek of despair, plunge headlong into the seething foam, his body, bruised and battered and hardly recognisable, being found many days later, calmly floating in some obscure nook maybe a mile or so away; and compared with these Scandinavian rivers the stream that now faced him was but a brooklet. All the same, he had never experienced such an intense fear and feeling of insecurity as now, when, stepping lightly over the first three stones, he landed on the centre one and gazed into the green, silent depths of the largest and deepest of the two pools that lay on either side of it. There was something curiously unnatural about this pool; he had never seen such a pronounced green in fresh water before, and its depth was in such marked contrast to the shallow, babbling water all around it. As he peered into it, a dark shadow seemed to well up to its surface, but he could trace no likeness in it to himself, and the trees were too far off for it to be produced by any one of them. He was asking himself how it could have come there, when his eyes wandered to the stone on which he was standing.

What an odd shape it was, nearly round and slightly convex, like the back of a turtle or some other queer amphibious creature, and it moved; he was positive of that, but it did not move with the rocking, vibrating movement he had witnessed in the picture; it moved with a furtive, sidelong, crawling action, as if it were alive. The sensation was unendurable. He turned to go, and, as he leaped through the air to the fourth stone, something whose attitude towards him he could not exactly define seemed to rise out of the green pool with astonishing celerity and leap with him. Arriving on the seventh and last stone, he was conscious of a strong restraining influence, an enigmatical something that seemed to be trying to pull him back, and it was only by exerting every atom of his will power that he succeeded in forcing himself forward. However, the moment his feet touched the bank and he was quite clear of the water, he was himself again. He turned and looked at the stone. It was absolutely motionless, while a stray sunbeam, gilding the surface of the silent pool, made it appear quite ridiculously cheerful. Vexed with himself for being such a fool, Casson now crossed the farm-yard and, going up to the house, knocked at the door. It was opened by a middle-aged woman, who might once have been the village belle, but who was now thin and worn.

" Yes," she said, running her eyes carefully over Casson's face and clothes. " What is it ? "

" Are you Mrs. Griffiths ? " Casson ejaculated. " I am a friend of Mr. Wotherall. I understand he once boarded with you."

" That's right," the woman replied. " He lived with me more than six months, and left two years ago last May. He didn't owe you anything, did he ? "

" Oh no," Casson replied quickly; " far from it. He and I were old schoolfellows. I saw a picture of his at the place I lunched at to-day, and, hearing he had been in the neighbourhood, I thought I would like to find out his present whereabouts."

" If you've come to inquire of me, I'm afraid you'll be disappointed," Mrs. Griffiths responded, " for I've neither seen him nor heard from him since he went away, and he would not leave any address for letters to be forwarded, as he said he had written to all his friends to tell them not to write here any more. A good many bills, but nothing else, came for him after he left, and those I have returned to the Dead Letter Office. He was very hard up, poor gentleman, and it's my opinion he didn't want his creditors to know what had become of him."

" I suppose he must have lost money then," Casson murmured, " for I always understood that his people were very comfortably fixed, and that he was an only child. Poor old Wotherall, I should so like to have met him again ! Do you still let rooms ? "

" Yes, sir," Mrs. Griffiths replied; " a top bed-room and parlour. The same two as Mr. Wotherall had. The last people that occupied them, a commercial traveller and his wife from Leeds, only left last week. Would you like to see them ? "

Casson acquiesced, and, liking the look of the rooms immensely, took them for a fortnight, which was all that remained of his seven weeks' holidays.

" It is a charming spot," he argued, " and I can easily amuse myself mooching about the fields or lying by the stream reading. Rest and quiet, and a plain, wholesome diet, such as one always gets at a farm, are just the very things I need."

He had a gorgeous tea that evening—strawberries, freshly gathered from the garden, cream, delicious butter and bread, none of that mysterious substitute that is palmed off on one nowadays in most of the London hotels and restaurants, but real home-made bread, which tasted far nicer than anything he had ever eaten in Bond Street or Piccadilly —and he enjoyed the meal so much, in fact, that he felt in a particularly amiable frame of mind, and thoroughly well satisfied with the world in general.

Presently he got up, intending to go out. He crossed the stone-flagged hall, and, passing the kitchen, the door of which was slightly open, he perceived Mrs. Griffiths busily engaged at a pastry-board rolling away as if for dear life. Wishing to be sociable, he called out, and as soon as she invited him in, opened up a conversation with her, inquiring how many cows she kept, how much land she rented, and had she a good crop of fruit. Whilst she was answering these questions, expatiating to no small degree on the trials and drawbacks of having to run a farm without a husband to look after it (she had, she remarked, with much emphasis and a dangerous approach to tears, been married twice, her first husband, "the best man as ever breathed," dying of consumption, and her second, a drunkard and a bad lot in every way, deserting her and going off to America, so she had always believed, with some other woman); whilst, I say, she was engaged telling him all this, he suddenly found himself gazing at an object hanging on the wall near the grandfather clock. It was a striped chocolate, white, and blue scarf, with the letters H.C. in white standing out in bold relief. He recognised the colours at once; they were the colours of Dempster's House at Harley. Evidently Wotherall had left the scarf behind as part of the personal effects that he had had to hand over to Mrs. Griffiths, in order to appease her indignation at his failure to produce the rent. Poor beggar, he must indeed have been hard pushed to part with so sacred a memento of his early life. Casson, like every other Harleyan, had the greatest reverence and affection for everything associated with the old School, the mere thought of which even now sent a thrill of genuine emotion through him.

"I see you have got a souvenir of my friend over there," he said, pointing to the scarf. "I suppose he made you a present of it when he left."

"What do you mean?" Mrs. Griffiths demanded, abruptly breaking off from her pastry-making

" A souvenir of your friend? I don't understand."

" I mean that scarf hanging on the wall there," Casson cried, again indicating with his hand its whereabouts. " It's my old School, or rather House, scarf. But what makes it blow about so? There doesn't seem to be any wind."

" House! scarf! colours ! " Mrs. Griffiths ejaculated. " I never heard tell of such things. You must be crazy. There's nothing on the wall saving that almanac that was given me by the grocer over in Coalbrookdale for a Christmas present. Have you never seen an almanac before ? "

" Not made of wool and behaving like that," Casson remarked. Then, going a few steps nearer, he gave vent to a loud exclamation of surprise. There was no scarf there at all, not the vestige of one, only a picture almanac representing an intensely silly-looking girl holding a lawn-tennis racket.

" My liver must be very wrong and I must be more than ordinarily bilious," Casson said. " I could have sworn it was a scarf."

" You're run down ; been working too hard, Mr. Casson," Mrs. Griffiths observed. " What you want is a rest. Go to bed early, and don't try your eyes over books and letter-writing."

Casson thanked her for her advice and, turning on his heels, left the kitchen. For one brief second he paused to look back. Mrs. Griffiths was staring after him, and in the depths of her large china-blue eyes, the pupils of which seemed to have grown to an unusual size, he read an expression of curiosity intermingled with fear.

The next few hours Casson spent lying on the grassy bank of the stream.   There was something wonderfully soothing in the constant rustling of the leaves of the big trees in the avenue, and the eternal babble, babble, babble of the water.   At times he construed the sounds into real sighings and whisperings, and fancied he could hear his name called, " Casson ! Casson ! Casson ! " very softly and plaintively, but occasionally with such reality that he started, and had to reassure himself earnestly that it was all imagination.   Then the shadows on the white soil of the avenue riveted his attention.   That they were only the shadows of the trees he had no doubt, and yet he queried every now and then if he had ever before seen shadows flit about and contort themselves in quite such an incomprehensible manner.   The emptiness of the avenue, too, seemed so emphasised.   Why was it so deserted ?   Why weren't there people about—living beings among those dark swaying trees and bushes like there were in the London parks ?   He did not know if he altogether liked the avenue now, when twilight was coming on.   His eyes had tricked him in the kitchen ; might they not trick him again out here, and in a rather more alarming manner ?   He would not look at the avenue again, not till it was broad daylight ; he would turn his attention to something else.   And then, of course, his eyes rested on the stepping-stones.   One, two, three, four, he counted. There was that confounded queer-shaped middle stone again, and that pool! How black and sinister they both looked in the semi-darkness! He would sound the pool in the morning and see if it was really as deep as he fancied. He turned away his eyes and tried to keep his attention concentrated on something else, but it was never any good, and in the end he invariably caught himself gazing at the stones, and particularly at the middle one. At last, tearing himself away with an effort, he went indoors and had supper, and at ten o'clock by his watch wended his way upstairs to bed. Just outside his door he suddenly pulled himself up sharply. Another step, and he felt he would have collided with something or, somebody, and yet, when he looked there was nothing—nothing save space. More convinced than ever now that there was something wrong either with the place or himself, Casson entered his room and proceeded to get into bed. The exertions of the day had made him tired, and he was soon asleep. He supposed he slept for about three hours, for he awoke with a start to hear the kitchen clock hurriedly strike two. His heart was beating furiously, and he had the most uncomfortable feeling that there was someone besides himself in the room. He fought against this feeling for some time, until, at last, unable to endure it any longer, he got out of bed, lit the candle, and searched the room thoroughly. The door was locked on the inside—he remembered locking it— and he was quite alone. " It must be nerves," he said, getting back into bed and blowing out the light. " A strong tonic is what I want. I will write to Dr. Joyce for one to-morrow. But I've never been afflicted with nerves before ! And in all consciousness I live simply enough ; so I don't know why I should suddenly develop biliousness." Then seized with a sudden desire to blow his nose, and recollecting that his handkerchief was on the chair by the bedside, he was putting out his hand to grope for it, when he felt it quietly thrust into his palm.

After that he pulled the bedclothes tightly over his head and kept them there till the morning. With the sunlight all doubts and uneasiness vanished, and Casson got out of bed fully convinced that all his experiences of the previous night were due to mere nervousness.

" I'm a Londoner," he argued, " and, not being used to the quiet and loneliness of these out-of-the-way places, I got the wind up."

Breakfast made him even more confident, and he went out into the yard in the cheeriest mood possible. After amusing himself watching the poultry, pigs, and other animals, he wandered through a wicket-gate into a field, and then through another field down to the stream. While he was threading his way back to the farm, through a mass of gorse and other undergrowth, he came upon a boy bending over a fishing-rod, busily intent on putting something red and raw—like uncooked meat —on a hook. " Whatever's that horrid-looking stuff," Casson said. " You'll never catch fish with bait like that. Why don't you use dough ? "

" 'Cos I know they like this best," was the

answer, and the boy looked up at Casson and grinned.

Casson was now so taken up with the boy's appearance that he forgot all about the bait. He had never seen such an unpleasant, queer, malshapen face before. The cranium was disproportionately large; the forehead and sides of the head immediately above and behind the ears were enormously developed; the chin was small and retreating; the ears, which stood very pronouncedly out from the head, were very big and pointed; the mouth huge; the eyes big, dark, and very heavily lidded; the skin yellow and unhealthy. The face was unprepossessing enough in repose, but when the lips opened and it smiled, the likeness to some ghoulish, froggish, and wholly monstrous kind of animal was increased a hundredfold, and Casson started back in dismay.

"Who are you?" he demanded, "and what right have you to fish here?"

"I like that—I do," the boy grunted. "Why, I've every right. I'm Ephraim Owen Lloyd. My mother, her you're staying with, was Mrs. Owen Lloyd before she married again and took the name of Griffiths. No right to fish here! You tell my mother that and see what she says." And, grinning wider than ever, he picked up the baited hook and flung it far into the stream.

Not wishing to have any further conversation with him, and feeling thoroughly disgusted and repelled, Casson walked on towards the stones. "Fancy being under the same roof with a young degenerate like that ! " he said to himself. " I wish now I hadn't decided to stay so long."

Slashing at the grass and other herbage with his stick—a trick Casson always resorted to when unsettled or annoyed—he reached the stones, and was about to turn into the yard when he received something of a surprise. A man in flannels, with a chocolate, white, and blue striped blazer, passed him by and, crossing the yard, vanished round an angle of the house. Casson did not see his face, but the back of his head, his figure, and walk at once recalled Wotherall. " If that's not Ralph," Casson exclaimed, " I'll eat my hat ! I wonder why he's come back ? It will give him a bit of a surprise when he sees me."

At the front door he ran into Mrs. Griffiths, who, with an apron full of French beans, was making for the kitchen.

" Have you seen him ? " Casson inquired.

" Seen who ? " Mrs. Griffiths rejoined.

" The man in the blazer, of course," Casson replied. " Mr. Wotherall, wasn't it ? "

" Mr. Wotherall ! " Mrs. Griffiths exclaimed, stopping short and staring hard at Casson. " You seem to have got Mr. Wotherall on the brain. Mr. Wotherall is nowhere near here—leastways, if he is, I've seen no signs of him."

" Why, there he is ! " Casson cried excitedly, pointing at a window, through which he saw a figure in the familiar Harleyan House blazer saunter slowly by. " That is Wotherall. He hasn't altered in the least. See, he's looking straight in here—at me! I'll go and speak to him!"

He ran to the door and threw it open. To his astonishment, there was no one there but young Ephraim Lloyd, who met his puzzled expression with an impudent leer.

"Where's Mr. Wotherall?" Casson cried. "What's become of him?"

The boy's countenance instantly underwent a change. "Mr. Wotherall!" he stammered. "What do you know of Mr. Wotherall?"

"Know of him?" Casson retorted angrily. "That's my business. He was here a few seconds ago, and now I can see no trace of him. Where is he, I say?"

By this time Mrs. Griffiths had deposited the beans on the kitchen table and joined the two at the door. "Take no notice of the gentleman," she said to Ephraim, "it's overwork. Been a-studying too hard. I've told him he must throw aside his books and letter-writing while he is here, and rest."

"Do you mean to tell me," Casson said "that neither of you saw a man in a blazer pass here just now?"

"Naw!" Ephraim drawled. "I ain't seen no one. There's no man in a blazer or in any other kind of thing anywhere about here. There's no man at all except yourself."

"That's right!" Mrs. Griffiths chipped in. "I told the gentleman so, only he won't believe me."

" I must have been dreaming, then," Casson replied reluctantly ; " but, at all events, I am awake now, and should like my dinner, Mrs. Griffiths, as soon as you can get it."

That ended the incident.   Casson retreated to his parlour, and the other two, after mumbling for awhile in the hall, retired together to the kitchen. The rest of the day passed uneventfully, and, once again, Casson found himself, candle in hand, wending his way upstairs to bed.

Just outside his door the same thing happened as on the previous night.   He thought he saw someone standing there, and pulled himself up sharply to avoid a collision.

Once inside his room he locked the door, and then looked everywhere to make sure no one was hiding.   That preliminary over, he stood for a while by the window smoking, then undressed, and got into bed.   Leaning on his elbow, he was about to blow out the candle, which was on the chair by his side, when there was a big puff and it was blown out for him.   No thought of investigating this time entered Casson's mind ; he dived deep under the bedclothes, and did not emerge till Mrs. Griffiths, almost thumping his door down, announced that his breakfast was on the table getting cold. After breakfast he went for a ramble in the fields, and as he had no desire to come in contact with Ephraim, towards whom he had taken a most violent dislike, he headed in a direction away from the stream.   He had not gone many yards, however, when he heard a cat screaming as if in fearful pain. Thinking some dog had got hold of it and was worrying it to death, and being very fond of cats, Casson at once made for the sounds, and in an open space, within a few yards of the stream, came upon a spectacle that he felt he could never forget, even if he lived a thousand years.

Tied down securely with cord to the top of a big wooden box was a black and white cat. Ephraim had hooked out one of its eyes, which was on the ground near his fishing-line, and was now about to hook out the other. The mystery of the bait Casson had seen him using the day before was thus explained.

With something like a howl of fury Casson rushed at Ephraim, and, seizing him by the scruff of his neck, thrashed him until his arms ached. Then flinging him on the ground with the remark, " You little devil, I hope I've killed you," he untied the cat. Weak with pain and loss of blood, the wretched animal had not the strength to move, and Casson, lifting it tenderly up, carried it to the house. Going straight into the kitchen, he showed it to Mrs. Griffiths.

" This is your son's work," he said. " I'm going to show it to the police at once, and I only hope he'll get a thorough good birching."

Mrs. Griffiths ceased what she was doing and looked at Casson defiantly.

" What do you want to interfere with Ephraim for ? " she remarked. " He ain't done nothing to you, has he ? "

" He's done nothing to me, perhaps," Casson

retorted, " but he's done something to this cat.
You can see for yourself."

" Well, he's only a boy," Mrs. Griffiths responded ;
" and if he has ill-treated the cat, there's not much
harm done. I expect it's the same cat that has
been after the chickens. The cats about here are
a perfect pest."

" That's no excuse for hooking their eyes out,"
Casson said hotly. " I intend leaving at once.
Here's a week's rent," and, taking some money
from his pocket, he deposited it on the table.

At that moment there were sounds of steps on
the gravel outside, loud hullabalooings, and Ephraim
burst into the kitchen.

" The gentleman's been hitting me," he bellowed.
" He struck me on the head and boxed my ears."

" You struck him ! " Mrs. Griffiths screamed,
her cheeks white with fury. " You dared to strike
him ! I'll have the law on you, see if I don't.
There, there, Ephraim, cease crying, and you shall
have what is left of that custard pudding you liked
so much yesterday."

This bribe apparently taking effect, Mrs. Griffiths
gave her offspring a final cuddle, and then veered
round with the intention of renewing an attack
upon Casson. Before she could open her mouth
to speak, however, there was another howling on
the part of Ephraim, and Casson, under cover of it
hurried off to his bedroom to collect his things.
As he went upstairs, both the boy and his mother
showered abuses on him, and he thought he heard
Ephraim say something to the effect that he wished

they could serve him as they had served someone else—the name of the someone else being drowned in a loud hush from Mrs. Griffiths, who afterwards began to speak very excitedly in Welsh.

On reaching his room Casson sought to revive the cat. He gave it some brandy from his flask, but the animal had been so badly mauled that all his efforts were in vain, and in a very few minutes it succumbed. He was thinking how he should carry it to the police station, when he heard a growl, and, looking round, saw a big black retriever dog, with a bright steel collar, standing on its hind legs, with its back towards him, gazing out of the window. Wondering whose dog it was, and what it was growling at, Casson went to the window, and, looking out, saw Mrs. Griffiths and the boy, each armed with a long pole, making off in the direction of the stream. Once or twice they peeped round, (whereupon Casson quickly hid himself behind the curtain), and then, apparently satisfied that they had not been seen, kept on following the course of the stream till they arrived at the stepping-stones. Crossing the first two, they stood on the third, and, thrusting the tops of their poles under the middle one, began to lever it up. Casson now thought it high time to depart. He felt convinced that they were setting some kind of trap for him, and that the exact nature of it was only known to themselves. Thanking his lucky stars that he had happened to look out of the window in time to see their little game, and determining to escape at once, avoiding the stepping-stones at all costs, he was preparing

14

to leave the room, when he suddenly thought of the dog. It was nowhere to be seen, and the door and the window were both shut. Where could it be ? He looked under the bed, in the cupboard, everywhere ; it was useless—the dog had vanished !

" The sooner I am out of this house," he muttered, as he ran downstairs and out at the kitchen door, " the better." And taking care, as he crossed the yard, to keep well out of sight of the stepping-stones, he ran in an opposite direction, without stopping for at least a mile.

Eventually he crossed the stream by a bridge, and found his way to a village, from whence he was able to proceed by train to Coalbrookdale. Arriving at the latter place, he went at once to the police, and telling them first of all about the cat, went on to narrate all that had happened to him at the farm. The police were not altogether unsympathetic ; they could, however, so they said, do nothing with regard to the cat without corroborative evidence, and, as to the other matter, they were afraid the law did not take cognizance of the superphysical, or suspicion founded on anything so immaterial as ghosts, although they themselves would not like to go as far as to deny their existence altogether. At length, being unable to prevail upon the police to do anything, Casson, by offering a handsome remuneration, persuaded two labourers to accompany him back to the stream. Arriving at the stepping-stones, they cautiously examined the middle one, and found it to be so poised that anyone standing on it would, by its unexpected tilt, suddenly be precipitated into a deep hole directly underneath it.

After considerable difficulty the stone was sufficiently moved on one side to enable the workmen to explore this hole, and at the bottom of it the skeletons of two men and a dog were discovered.

There was nothing on the one skeleton that could in any way help to identify it ; but remnants of clothes, ragged and rotten, still adhered to the other, and from the name engraven on a card-case in the pocket of the coat, which tallied with the initials on the undergarments and a signet ring, there was little doubt but that the remains were those of Ralph Wotherall. [From subsequent inquiries it was ascertained that the friends and relatives of Ralph Wotherall had heard from him immediately prior to the time he was supposed to have left Stepping-Stone Farm, but had not heard from him since, a fact to which they had attributed little importance, as Wotherall, on more than one occasion, had suddenly decided to go abroad, where he had stayed for a couple of years or so without letting anyone know where he was or what he was doing. The story, they said, of his being so hard up as to be unable to pay the rent could be discredited by his solicitors, who would testify to the fact that they had but recently invested a large sum of money for him, from which he was deriving a not inconsiderable income.] A steel collar bearing the initials R. L. W. was found round the neck of the third skeleton, and as several people remembered having seen a big black retriever with Wotherall while he was staying at the farm, it was pretty certain that the canine remains were those of his dog. However, Mrs. Griffiths, who appeared to be quite as astonished as anyone at the discovery of the skeletons, still stuck to her original story that Wotherall had left the neighbourhood, taking his dog with him, and against her statements Casson could only reiterate his surmises. He was quite certain that Mrs. Griffiths and her evil-faced son were guilty of murder, that, having done away with Wotherall and some other man by means of the stepping-stone, they had deliberately set the same death-trap for him, and that he had only been saved from falling into it by the apparition of his old friend's dog ; but he could not, of course, expect the police to work up a case, which, from their point of view, rested upon such an unsubstantial foundation, and as on examination the skeleton showed no evidence of foul play, there was no alternative, the usual verdict of " Death from mis-adventure " had to be returned.

CHAPTER XIII

THE PINES

" Who is the most interesting person in this institution ? " my friend Dr. Custance remarked, repeating my words. " If you mean from your point of view—ghosts, I should say Dacre, George Richard Dacre. He is pretty old now—close upon seventy, and very possibly you have never heard of him. The case, with which he was somewhat closely connected, took place in Cumberland about forty years ago, and the spot is still said to be haunted. If you would like to hear all about it, come along, and I will introduce you to him."

Custance led me into a room, where an old man, with a glistening bald head and white beard, sat, leaning back in his chair, and examining his hands with an air of strange intensity.

" Mr. Dacre," Custance remarked, " I have brought you a visitor, a Mr. Elliot O'Donnell, who is very interested in the supernatural, and would much like to hear some of your experiences."

The old man raised his eyes ; they did not look at me, but beyond, far beyond, into a world that seemed known only to himself.

" I have only had one experience," he said, " and that was a long while ago ; so long that, at times, it seems as if it must have happened to me in another incarnation, when I was something out of doors—a pine or an elm—something growing in a wood. I can still, occasionally, smell resin, after one of those long hot summers we used to have, —seventy or eighty years ago,—and occasionally hear the wind, the deliciously cool, evening breezes, rustling and sighing, as it were, through my branches and fanning my perspiring bark. Sit down, and I will tell you all about it.

.   .   .   .

" It was a cold night. Rain had been falling steadily not only for hours but days—the ground was saturated. As I walked along the country lane, the slush splashed over my boots and trousers. To my left was a huge stone wall, behind which I could see the nodding heads of pines ; and through them the wind was rushing, making a curious whistling sound—now loud, now soft—roaring and gently murmuring. The sound fascinated me. I fancied it might be the angry voice of a man and the plaintive pleading of a woman, and then, a weird chorus of unearthly beings, of grotesque things that stalked across the moors and crept from behind huge boulders. Nothing but the wind was to be heard. I stood and listened to it. I could have listened for hours, for I felt in harmony with my surroundings—lonely. The moon showed itself at intervals from behind the scudding clouds and lighted up the open landscape to my right. A gaunt hill covered with rocks, some piled up pyramidically, others strewn here and there ; a few trees with naked arms tossing about and looking distressfully thin beside the more stalwart boulders ; a sloping field or two, a couple of level ones, crossed by a tiny path ; and the lane, where I stood. The scenery was desolate—not actually wild, but sad and forlorn ; and the wood by my side lent an additionally weird aspect to the place, which was pleasing to me.

" Suddenly I heard a sound—a sound, familiar enough at other times ; but, at this hour, and in this place, everything seemed different. A woman was coming along the road—a woman in a dark cloak, with a basket under her arm ; and the wind was blowing her skirts about her legs.

" I looked at the trees. One singularly gaunt and fantastic one appalled me. It had long, gnarled arms, and two of them ended in bunches of twigs like hands—yes, they were exactly like hands—huge, murderous-looking hands, with bony fingers. The moonlight played over and around me—I was bathed in it. I had no business to be on the earth —my proper place was in the moon. I no longer thought it—I knew it. The woman was close at hand. She stopped at a little wicket gate leading into the lane skirting the northern boundary of the wood. I felt angry ; what right had she to be there, interrupting my musings with the moon ! The tree with the human hands appeared to agree. I saw anger in the movements of its branches—anger, which soon blazed into fury. It gave a mighty bend towards her, as if longing to rend her in pieces.

" I followed the woman ; and the wind howled louder and louder through those rustling leaves.

" How long I scrambled on I do not know. As soon as the moonlight left me, I fell into a kind of slumber — a delicious trance, broken only by the restless murmurings, the sighings and groanings of the wind. Sweeter music I never heard. Then came a terrible change. The charm of my thoughts was broken—I awoke from my reverie.

" A terrific roar broke on my ears, and a perfect hurricane of rain swept through the wood. I crept cold and shivering beneath the shelter of the trees. To my surprise a hand fell on my shoulder : it was a man, and, like myself, he shivered.

" ' Who are you ? ' he whispered, in a strangely hoarse voice. ' Who are you ? Why are you here ? '

" ' You wouldn't believe me if I told you,' I replied, shaking off the man's grasp.

" ' Well,—tell me,' he rejoined ; ' for God's sake tell me." He was frightened—trembling with fright. Could it be the storm, or was it—was it those trees ?

" I told him then and there why I had trespassed. I was fascinated—the wind—and the trees—had led me thither.

" ' So am I,' he whispered ; ' I am fascinated. It is a long word, but it describes my sentiments. What did the wind sound like ? '

" I told him. He was a poor, common man, and had no poetical ideas. The wildly romantic had never interested him—he was but an ignorant labouring man.

"'Sounded like sighing, groaning, and so on?' he said, repeating my words, and shifting uneasily from one foot to another. He was cold, horribly cold. 'Was that all?'

"'Yes, of course. Why ask?' I replied. Then I laughed. This stupid, sturdy son of toil had been scared; to him the sounds had been those of his moorland bogies—things he had dreaded in his infancy. I told him so. He didn't like to hear me make fun of him. He didn't like my laugh, and he persisted: 'Was that all you heard?'

"Then I grew impatient, and asked him to explain what he meant.

"'Well,' he said, 'I thought I heard a scream,— a cry. Just as if some one had jumped out on some one else and taken them unawares. Maybe it was the wind—only the wind. But it had an eerie sound.'

"The man was nervous. The storm had frightened away whatever little wit he may have possessed.

"'Come, let us be going,' I said, moving off in the direction of the wall. I wanted to find a new exit; I was tired of paths.

"The man kept close to me. I could hear his teeth chatter. Accidentally his hand brushed against mine. His flesh was icy cold. He gave a cry as if a snake had bitten him. Then the truth flashed through me. The man was mad. His terror, his strange manner of showing it, and now this sudden shrinking from me revealed it all—he was mad—the moon and trees had done their work.

" ' I'm not going that way,' he said, ' come along with me. I want to see which of the trees it was that cried.'

" His voice was changed ; he seemed suddenly to have grown stranger. There was no insanity in his tone now. But I knew the cunning of the insane, and I feared to anger him, so I acquiesced. What an idea ! One of the trees had cried ! Did he mean the wind ?

" He grew sullen when I jeered at him. He led me to a little hollow in the ground, and I noticed the prints of several feet in the wet mud. Then I saw something which sent the cold blood to my heart. A woman bathed in blood lay before me. Somehow she was familiar to me. I looked again— then again. Yes, there was the dark shawl, the basket—broken, it was true, with the contents scattered ; but it was the same basket. It was the woman I had seen coming down the road.

" ' My God, whatever is this ! ' The man by my side spoke. He swayed backwards and forwards on his feet, his face white and awful in the moonlight. He was sick with terror. ' Oh God, it is horrible — horrible ! " Then, with a sudden earnestness and a crafty look in his eyes, he bent over her.

" ' Who is it ? ' he cried. ' Who is the poor wretch ? '

" I saw him peer into her face, but he didn't

touch her—he dreaded the blood. Then he started back, his eyes filled with such savageness as I had never seen in any man's before. He looked a devil—he was a devil. ' It's my wife ! ' he shrieked. ' My wife ! ' His voice fell and turned into what sounded like a sob. ' It's Mary. She was coming back to Helvore. It was her cry. There—see it—confound you! You have it on your arm—your coat—all over you.'

" He raised his hand to strike me. The moonlight fell on it—a great coarse hand—and I noticed, with a thrill of horror, a red splash on it. It was blood. The man was a murderer. He had killed his wife, and, with all the cunning of the madman, was trying to throw the guilt on me.

" I sprang at him with a cry of despair. He kicked and bit, and tried to tear my arms from his neck ; but somehow I seemed to have ten times my usual strength.

" And all the time we struggled a sea of faces waved to and fro, peering down at us from the gaunt trees above.

" He gave in at length. I was no longer obliged to hold him with an iron grip, and help came eventually in the shape of a policeman, who seemed to grasp the situation quite easily. There had been a murder ; the man I had secured was known to him. He was a labouring man of unsteady habits ; he had been drinking, had met and quarrelled with his wife. The rest was to be seen in the ghastly heap before us.

" The wretch had no defence. He seemed

dazed, and eyed the bloodstains on his face and clothes in a stupid kind of way.

" I slipped five shillings into the policeman's hand when we parted. He thanked me and pocketed the money ; he knew his position and mine too ; I was a gentleman, and a very plucky one at that. So I thought as I walked back to my rooms ; yet I lay awake and shuddered as visions of the nodding heads of pines passed before me ; and from without, across the silent lanes and fields, there rose and fell again the wailing of a woman—a woman in distress.

. . . .

" The murder in the wood was an event in Helvore. The people were unused to such tragedies, and it afforded them something to talk about for many weeks. The evidence against the husband was conclusive. He had been caught red-handed, he was an habitual drunkard, and he paid the penalty for his crime in the usual manner.

" I left Helvore. I had seen enough of Cumberland and thirsted for life in London once again. Yet, often at night, the sighing of the wind in the trees sounded in my ears, bidding me visit them once more.

" One day as I was sitting by my fire with a pile of books at my side, taking life easily, for I had nothing to do but to kill time, my old friend, Frank Leethwaite, looked me up. He had been at Sedbergh with me in the far-off eighties, and he was the only friend of the old set with whom I had been out of touch.

" He had not altered much, in spite of a moustache and a fair sprinkling of white hairs. I should have known him had I met him anywhere. He was wearing an Albert coat, and his face was red with healthy exercise.

" ' How are you, old chap ? ' he exclaimed, shaking hands in the hearty fashion of true friendship.

" I winced, for he had strong hands.

" ' Fit enough,' I said, ' only a bit bored.' But you—well, you look just the same, and fresh as a daisy.' I gave him the easy-chair.

" ' Oh, I'm first rate—plenty of work. I'm a journalist, you know. It's a bit of a grind, but I'm taking a holiday. You look pale. Your eyes are bad ? '

" I told him they got strained if I read much.

" ' I daresay you will think me mad,' he went on, ' but I'm going to ask you rather a curious question. I remember you used to be fond of ghosts and all sorts of queer things.'

" I nodded. We had had many discussions on such subjects, in my study at school.

" ' Well, I'm a member of the New Supernatural Investigation Society.'

" I smiled doubtfully. " Well, you can't say it has discovered much. The name is high-sounding, but that is all.'

" ' Never mind. Some day, perhaps, we shall show the public what we can do.

" Leethwaite lit a cigarette, puffed away in silence for a few seconds, and then went on :

" ' I am undertaking a little work for the Society now ! '

" ' Where ? '

" ' In Cumberland. Ever been there ? '

" I nodded. Leethwaite was very much at his ease.

" ' Been to Helvore ? '

" I knew by instinct he would mention the place.

" He thought I looked ill, and told me I had been overdoing it.

" ' It is merely a case of " flu," ' I assured him. ' I had it six weeks ago, and still feel the effects.'

(" The woman in the hollow was before me. I saw again her shabby shawl and the blood round her throat.)

" ' There was a murder down there a short time ago.'

" ' I heard of it,' I remarked casually. ' It was a wife murder, I believe.'

" ' Yes, just a common wife murder, and the fellow was caught and hanged.'

" ' Then why the ghost ? '

" ' Well, that is the odd part of it,' Leethwaite said slowly, leaning back in his chair, his long legs stretched out.

" ' I have heard from two Helvore residents that screams have been heard in the wood about twelve o'clock at night. Not the time for practical jokers, and the Cumberland peasantry are too superstitious to try their pranks in unsavoury spots. Besides, from what I have heard, the spot is not only unsavoury, it is singularly uncanny.'

" ' They haven't seen anything ? ' I asked.

" ' No, only heard the cries, and they are so terribly realistic that no one cares to pass the place at night ; indeed, it is utterly banned. I mentioned the case to old Potters—you must have heard of him, he used to write a lot for the *Gentleman's Magazine*— and he pressed me to go down and investigate. I agreed ; then I thought I would look you up. Do you remember your pet aversion in the way of ghosts ? '

" I nodded. ' Yes, and I still have the aversion. I think locality exercises strange influence over some minds. The peaceful meadow scenery holds no lurking horrors in its bosom ; but in the lonely moorlands, full of curiously moulded boulders, one sees, or fancies one sees, grotesque creatures, odd and ill-defined as their surroundings. As a child I had a peculiar horror of those tall, odd-shaped boulders, with sneering faces—featureless, it is true, but sometimes strangely resembling the faces of humans and animals. I believe the wood may be haunted by something of this nature—terrible as the trees.'

" ' You know the wood ? '

" ' I do. And I know the trees.'

" Again in my ears the wind rushed, as it had on that memorable night.

" ' Will you come with me ? '

" Leethwaite eyed me eagerly. The same old affection he had once entertained for me was

ripening in his eyes ; indeed it had always remained there. Should I go ? An irresistible
impulse seized me, a morbid craving to look once
more at the blood-stained hollow, to hear again the
wind. I looked out of the window ; the sky was
cold and grey. There were rows and rows of
chimneys—chimneys everywhere—and an ocean of
dull, uninviting smoke. I began to hate London
and to long for the countless miles of blue
sea, and the fresh air of the woods. I assented
though my better judgment would have had me
refuse.

"‘ Yes, I replied, I will go. As to the ghost,
it may be there, but it is not what you think ; it
is not the apparition of a man. It may be, in
part, like a man, but it is one of those cursed
nightmares I have always had. I shall see it,
hear it shriek—and if I drop dead from fright,
you, old man, will be to blame.’

" Leethwaite was an enthusiast, and psychical
adventure always allured him. He would run
the risk of my weak heart, he said, and have me
with him.

" A thousand times I prepared to go back on
my word ; a thousand tumultuous emotions of
some impending disaster rushed through me. I
felt on the border of an abyss, dark and hopeless ;
I was pushed on by invisible and unfriendly hands.
I knew I must fall ; I knew that those black depths
would engulf me eternally. I took the plunge.
We talked over Sedbergh days, and arranged our
train to the North. Leethwaite looked very

boyish, I thought, as he rose to go, and stood smiling in the doorway.

"He was all kindness; I liked him more than ever. And yet, somehow, as we stood looking at one another, a grey shadow swept around him, and an icy pang shot through my heart.

.   .   .   .

"It was night once more, and the moonlight poured in floods from over the summit of the knoll where the uncanny boulders lay. Every object stood silhouetted against the dark background. A house, with its white walls, stood grim and silent; the paths running in various directions up and alongside the hill were made doubly clear by the whiteness of the beams that fell on them. There were no swift clouds, no mists to hide the brilliance of the stars, and it was nearly midnight. The air was cold, colder than is usual at Helvore, and I shivered. Leethwaite stood by my side. I glanced apprehensively at him. Why did he stand in the moonlight? What business had he there? I laughed, but I fear there was but little mirth in the sound.

"'I wish you would stop that infernal noise,' he said; 'I am pretty nervous as it is.'

"'All right,' I whispered; 'I won't do it again.'

"But I did, and he edged sharply away from me. I looked over his head. There was the gaunt tree with the great hands. I fancied once again the branches were fingers. I told him so.

"'For God's sake, man, keep quiet," he replied.

15

You are enough to upset any one's nerves.' He looked at his watch for the hundredth time. ' It's close on the hour.'

" I again looked at the trees and listened. Suddenly, although there had been absolute silence before, I heard a faint breathing sound, a very gentle murmur. It came from over the distant knoll. At first very soft and low, but gradually getting louder and louder, it rushed past us into the wood beyond. I saw once more the great trees rock beneath it ; and again I heard those voices—those of the woman and the man.

" Leethwaite looked ill, very ill, I thought. I touched him on the arm. ' You are not frightened,' I said ; ' you—a member of the New Supernatural Investigation Society ? '

" ' Something is going to happen,' he gasped. ' I feel it—I know it. We shall see the murder— we shall know the secret of death. What is that ? '

" Away in the distance the tap-tapping of shoes came through the still night air. Tap—tap—tap, down the path from the knoll.

" I clutched Leethwaite by the arm. ' You think you will see the murder, do you ? And the murderer ! '

" Leethwaite didn't answer. His breath came in gasps ; he looked about him like a man at bay.

" ' And the murderer ! Ha ! It comes from there. See, it is looking at us from those trees. It is all arms and legs ; it has no human face. It will drop to the earth, and then we shall see what happens.'

" Tap, tap, tap—the steps grew louder—nearer and nearer they came. The great shadows stole down, one by one, to meet them. I looked at Leethwaite. He was fearfully expectant ; so was I.

" A woman came tripping along the path. I knew her in an instant—there was the shabby shawl, the basket on her arm—it was the same. She approached the wicket.

" I looked at Leethwaite. He was spellbound with fear. I touched his arm. I dragged him with me. ' Come,' I whispered, ' we shall see which of us is right. You think the ghostly murderer will resemble us—will resemble men. It will not. Come.'

" I dragged him forward. He would have fled, but I was firm. We passed through the gate—we followed the figure as it silently glided on. We turned to the left. The place grew very dark as the trees met overhead. I heard the trickling of water and knew we were close to the ditch.

" I gazed intently at the pines. When would the horror drop from them ? A sickly terror laid hold of me. I turned to fly.

" To my surprise Leethwaite stopped me. He was all excitement. ' Wait,' he hissed. ' Wait. It is you who are afraid. Hark ! It is twelve o'clock.' And as he spoke, the clock of the parish church slowly tolled midnight. Then the end came. An awful scream rang out; so piercing and so full of terror that I felt the blood in my heart stand still.   But no figure dropped from the pines. Not from the pines, but from behind the woman a form darted forward and seized her by the neck. It tore at her throat with its hands, it dragged and hurried her into the moonlight ; and then, oh damning horror, I saw its face !—it was my own."

Printed in Great Britain
by Amazon

40058643R00131